CROQUET

Steven Boga

STACKPOLE BOOKS

Copyright © 1995 by Stackpole Books

Published by
STACKPOLE BOOKS
5067 Ritter Road
Mechanicsburg, PA 17055
www.stackpolebooks.com

Printed in the United States of America

10 9 8 7 6 5 4 3 2

First edition

Cover design by Caroline Miller

Library of Congress Cataloging-in-Publication Data

Boga, Steve, 1947–
    Croquet / Steven Boga. — 1st ed.
        p.   cm.
    ISBN 0-8117-2489-1 (pbk. : alk. paper)
    1. Croquet. I. Title
GV931.B64 1995
796.35'4—dc20   94-45855
                                                                          CIP

    ISBN 978-0-8117-2489-0

CONTENTS

....

INTRODUCTION

....

*It's not the same game. It's an absolutely
different game, that's the trouble. It's a different game and everyone thinks it's a kids'
game or an old lady's game or some damn
thing.*

—Darryl F. Zanuck

I agree with former Hollywood mogul and croquet fanatic Darryl
Zanuck that croquet is a highly misunderstood game.
Although popular at clubs and in American backyards, it receives
only a tiny fraction of the attention it deserves. There are, in my
opinion, three glaring reasons for this:

1. Croquet doesn't "do" television.
2. The players wear white.
3. It's more mental than physical.

1. TV. Okay, *Wide World of Sports* would get a few snotty
    complaints if it aired an entire ninety-minute champi-
    onship croquet match. But what is life without risk?
    Write to ABC and demand equal time for croquet. Call
    the newspapers and ask for the croquet box scores.

2. Whitewear. Croquet is widely perceived as a sport for
    the hoity-toity rich. Books and movies perpetuate this
    image, but what really drives it home is the tradition of
    players wearing white. The game has loosened up some-
    what—tournament attire today is only "predominantly
    white" and Adidas and Reebok are the shoes of choice—
    but croquet players still have a clean, uptight image.
    They would probably draw bigger crowds if they had

cheerleaders or if the players wore knee pads and eye black.

I make light to drive home this point: Croquet is not owned exclusively by the pampered and privileged. With its backyard origins, croquet is in fact a game for the masses. Its players hail from disparate points on the socioeconomic scale. Not all their collars are white. Wayne Rodoni, a top-ranked American player, is a sheet-metal worker. Tony Stephens, mallet champion from New Zealand, is a dairy farmer. At the 1994 World Croquet Championship, not one of the twenty-eight competitors was a member of the idle rich.

3. Mind vs. body. Sure, croquet is a lot less physical than the biggies—baseball, basketball, and football—but it's only slightly less physical than golf, a sport to which it is often compared. Yet while golf flourishes—as both a televised and participant sport—croquet languishes in relative anonymity. Both emphasize brisk walking; both are big on putting (golfers take about half of their strokes on the green; croquet players all of theirs). But putting is not nearly as interesting or strategy-packed as hitting different-colored croquet balls.

Croquet's real PR problem, at the top level, is its complexity. It's a thinking game more than an action game. Mental acuity is more important than muscles— it can take years to plumb the strategic depths of top-flight croquet. On the other hand, in the backyard game strategy takes a back seat to banging balls around, so the fun starts right from the get-go.

Croquet is a uniquely social game, suitable for any number of people in the "eat drink and be merry" mode. Ideal for gatherings of family or friends, it can be played with equal facility by both sexes, the young and the old, the weak and the strong, the fit and the fat. It can, in fact, be played by anyone with enough vigor to swing a mallet and hit a stationary ball a few feet. Moreover, there are several ways to handicap play, making it more fun for weaker players. In reality, croquet is not elitist, but one of the most democratic games of all time. After all, all you need is a lawn.

In the chapters that follow, you will learn about croquet strategy and technique. Before you can make sense of that, however, you have to understand the basics of play, including the vocabulary. Pay particular attention to the italicized buzz words in the following paragraphs. They are defined in more detail in the glossary.

Whether you are playing nine-wicket or six-wicket croquet, the goal is to score points by hitting balls with a mallet through a course of *hoops*. It is best for two or four players and can be played by teams or individuals. Whoever finishes the course first or scores the most points in an agreed time is the winner.

The sides alternate play. The *striker* is the person whose turn it is to hit. The striker's turn consists initially of one *stroke*, but it is extended if that stroke either a) scores a *wicket* or hits a *stake* (one *bonus stroke*), or b) *roquets* (hits) another ball (two bonus strokes).

The striker's ball is entitled to roquet any ball upon which it is *alive*, thereby earning two extra shots. After the roquet, the striker's ball is moved *(ball-in-hand)* to where the roqueted ball came to rest in order to take the first *(croquet)* stroke of the two it has earned. A striker is only rewarded for roqueting a ball upon which the striker's ball is alive. The striker's ball becomes *dead* on any ball so hit and may not hit it again until the striker's ball scores its next wicket or stake point. If the striker's ball does hit a ball upon which it is dead, both balls are replaced and the striker's turn ends.

• • • • • •

Special thanks to the players who gave of their time to help make this book possible: Barrie Chambers, Wayne Rodoni, Neil Spooner, Tony Stephens, Rhys Thomas, and Charlie Smith. Also, my gratitude to Garth Eliassen, publisher of the National Croquet Calendar; to Bob Sumwalt, nine-wicket chairman; to Dan and Jan O'Connell for opening their courts to me; and to Anne Frost, Dean Reinke, and the staff at the United States Croquet Association.

HISTORY OF CROQUET

··

As each player goes through the first hoop,
as he undergoes a metamorphosis . . . the
male antagonist becomes a creature too vile
for language. The decency of womanhood
has disappeared by the third hoop.
　　　　　　　　　—*Living Age,* circa 1898

The headwaters of croquet are murky. Historians have trouble even agreeing on the origin of the name. The *Oxford English Dictionary* traces the word to the Old North French *croche,* meaning shepherd's crook. The Irish claim it is from the Gaelic *cluiche,* pronounced "crooky" and meaning play.

The game is said to have originated in the 1300s, when peasants in southern France made hoops by bending willow branches and began hitting balls through them with hooked mallets that resembled shepherds' crooks.

This ancestral version of croquet—called *paille maille,* later *pall mall*—made the leap across the English Channel, and by the seventeenth century it was a court favorite of Britain's Charles II. Players used a curved club, wooden balls, and two hoops. The court was made of powdered cockleshells and the wickets were festooned with flowers. Those were the days.

Croquet died out in England, but caught fire again in Ireland around 1830. Twenty years later, it made a comeback in England, demonstrating both its competitive and social appeal to the Victorians. Competitively, it was unique, allowing men and women to compete equally, maybe for the first time. It was also good at parties, and after-dinner croquet fests became all the rage, eventually finding appeal in India, Australia, New Zealand, and the United States. For a time, croquet enthusiasts far outnumbered their tennis counterparts. Croquet sets were mandatory equipment on every estate and in every city park.

Some historians credit Louisa May Alcott's novel *Little Women,* which carries a description of croquet, with spurring interest in the game.

The sport's first rulebook, *Routledge's Handbook of Croquet,* was published in England in 1861. In 1863, Captain Mayne Reid discussed the social impact of croquet in his book *Croquet: A Treatise and Commentary.* He argued that croquet, a character-enhancing alternative to warfare, was good for society, especially if young women could be kept from the young men who played it. It was improper, he continued, for men and women to compete on common ground because it could lead to immoral conduct. In Victorian England, croquet was hot stuff.

In 1864, London equipment manufacturer John Jaques printed 25,000 rulebooks to accompany his croquet sets. So explosive was the sport that Jaques printed 50,000 rulebooks the following year.

A tournament was held in 1867 in Evesham, Worcestershire, that came to be known as the first Open Championship. The All-England Croquet Club (AECC) was formed in 1868. Croquet also caught on in the United States. The Newport (Rhode Island) Croquet Club was active by 1865; the National American Croquet Association by 1882. The rich were the first to call the game their own, but soon civic groups joined the bandwagon. It seemed no one was immune to croquet's allure. President Rutherford B. Hayes spent six dollars of taxpayers' money on a set of fancy croquet balls, an act of profligacy that enraged the Democratic opposition but permitted the president to tune up his game.

The author of the 1865 handbook of the Newport Croquet Club attributed the game's popularity to its inherent challenge: "Whist exercises the memory and the power of calculating probabilities, chess the imagination and the faculty of abstract reasoning, but croquet, though it taxes these mental capacities less, combines them with the delights of out-of-doors exercise and social enjoyment, fresh air and friendship—two things which are of all others most effective for promoting happiness." An 1871 Milton Bradley handbook touted the game as the perfect match for a young, achievement-minded nation: "When we work or fight, we work and fight harder than any other people," it boasted. "We should be as enthusiastic in our play."

Others had a different perspective. Self-appointed guardians of the public morality railed against croquet for permitting young ladies to do sport with young men. The combination of co-ed exercise and fresh air, they fretted, would cause young men to leer at women in decidedly un-Christian ways. The sport also was frequently associated with drinking and gambling. In 1898, one bluenose publication railed that "the game is the gaping jaw of Hades. It would be well if the enthusiasm of the clergy and the laity were enlisted for suppressing the immoral practice of croquet."

With such sentiment on the rise, croquet was banned in Boston. Other municipalities discarded their croquet equipment. In the 1870s, lawn tennis, which had the common decency to separate its players by a net, supplanted croquet in popularity. The first croquet boom became the first croquet bust.

In the late nineteenth century, England "re-rediscovered" croquet. In 1896, the United All-England Croquet Association was founded. Known today simply as the Croquet Association (CA), it still rules the game in England.

A U.S. revival occurred in 1899, when a group of players met in Norwich, Connecticut, to revise the old Routledge rules and revitalize the game. Using a nine-wicket version, they standardized court and hoop size and reduced from four to two the number of balls each player played.

The Americans introduced their unique nine-wicket game at the 1904 Olympics in St. Louis. Largely because no one else in the world played that version, the Americans won the first and only gold medal in Olympic croquet.

If the first golden age of croquet occurred in Victorian England, the second took place in the 1920s and 1930s among American socialites. It became the favorite sport of the literary and theater sets. On the East Coast, Herbert Bayard Swope, executive editor of the *New York World,* and writer Alexander Woolcott discovered their common passion for the game. Swope owned a Long Island estate, complete with an expansive croquet lawn. It was there that Woolcott introduced dramatists Moss Hart and

George S. Kaufman, poet Dorothy Parker, and other members of the legendary Algonquin Roundtable literary group to the splendor of nine-wicket, two-stake, no-boundary croquet.

Another avid member of the group was Harpo Marx, who later helped popularize the sport on the West Coast. So devoted to the game was Harpo that he converted a spare bedroom into an air-conditioned storeroom to house his croquet equipment. On one occasion, he disrupted a meeting between Woolcott and Eleanor Roosevelt by banging croquet balls in the hallway outside Woolcott's apartment.

The matches on Swope's estate were played with a zeal that is hard to fathom—until you know that oodles of money was often riding on the outcome. Harpo recounted a match that he and Swope completed while the governor of New York, Al Smith, was kept waiting on the telephone. Another match was incomplete when darkness fell, so Swope had his guests ring the court with their cars and turn their lights on. Five cars suffered dead batteries, but it was, at least for Swope, a small price to pay for finishing the match.

Woolcott, especially, seems to have lived and died by his croquet game. "My doctor forbids me to play unless I win," he would declare. His friends went so far as to make a movie satirizing his fierce competitiveness. At the end of the movie, Woolcott is burned at the stake for kicking his croquet partner.

Another croquet devotee was diplomat Averell Harriman. Once during a Thanksgiving storm, when snow threatened to curtail a match, he hired eight men with tools to keep the courts clean.

On the West Coast, croquet was embraced by movie moguls Darryl Zanuck and Samuel Goldwyn. Both had grandiose courts. Zanuck's greensward in Palm Springs sported a fountain in the center, a formidable obstacle for visiting players. When Goldwyn could no longer play golf, he had two tournament-quality lawns installed on his Beverly Hills estate. He was renowned for a shot called "Sam's crush," in which he unfairly pushed the ball through the wicket. There is no record of any complaints.

Other movie people who took up croquet included Gig Young, Louis Jordan, Howard Hawks, Tyrone Power, George Sanders, and the relocated Harpo Marx. Gambling was an important part of the ritual, with bets of $10,000 or more.

Although Louis Jordan was said to be the best player of the group, Darryl Zanuck was the fiercest competitor. Called "the terrible-tempered Mr. Bang," he possessed, in Moss Hart's opinion, "the true croquet spirit. He trusts no one but himself; never concedes—no matter how far behind he may be—and he hates his opponents with an all-enduring hate."

Despite all the movie-star hype, the East Coasters vociferously insisted that they were number one. To settle the matter, the first (and last) East-West Croquet Championship was held in Palm Springs in 1946. Three hundred Hollywood bigwigs were in attendance. The West won the first game and the East the second, setting up a rubber match that lasted long into the night. As Moss Hart remembered, "Cheating is as much a part of croquet as it is of poker, but in the dark it got out of control."

Eleven hours after they started, the East claimed a hard-fought victory. It was said that they complained bitterly about the undersized victor's cup.

"The British form of croquet is a better game than ours . . . more sportsmanlike. Ours is a more strategic game and far more emotional. In our game you do what you call 'destroying your opponent.' The British don't go so far. They wouldn't think of doing things like some of our former leaders, like the late Alexander Woolcott. Why, he had his court beside a lake and thought nothing of knocking a guest's ball in the water. That sometimes caused trouble."

—Averell Harriman

When Zanuck retired from competition, Goldwyn's court was the only remaining quality greensward on the West Coast. Then, when Goldwyn took to his deathbed, his wife turned off the water to the courts, effectively abolishing play. She feared Sam would become overexcited listening to his friends outside playing the game he loved.

In the sixties, croquet experienced another revival, particularly on the East Coast. Several croquet clubs were founded in New York City, Westhampton, Palm Beach, and Bermuda. By 1966, the Americans had progressed sufficiently to send a three-man team to London to challenge the English. Although they were soundly thrashed, they picked up some valuable tips, not the least of which was the home-court advantage. The following year, the English team visited Long Island, where they were surprised to encounter the nine-wicket, two-post version of the game common only in American backyards. The competition ended in a three-to-three tie. In 1968, the series returned to England, where the Americans were given a bitter dose of reality: a return to British rules and an eight-to-zero defeat.

Several independent clubs banded together in 1977 to form the United States Croquet Association (USCA). With that, the game took another giant step forward. The USCA encouraged the formation of local croquet clubs, and soon such clubs were springing up all over. Some were tiny (membership of the Chipmunk Hollow Croquet Club in Franklin, New York: one family), some had frustratingly short seasons (the Anchorage Croquet Club held almost all matches in June between 3:30 A.M. and 11:30 P.M.), but they all shared a passion for the game. As of this writing, more than three hundred croquet clubs are members of the USCA.

In 1986, the American Croquet Association was founded to promote international-rules croquet in the United States. In 1993, the United States was invited for the first time to compete against Great Britain, Australia, and New Zealand in the Mac-Robertson Shield, the most prestigious international croquet competition. Playing against the finest players in the world, the Americans finished in fourth place. But the invitation alone suggests good things ahead for croquet in the United States.

COURT AND EQUIPMENT

....

*There are really two great moments for a
croquet player, aside from winning a game.
The first is when he is introduced to croquet. The second is when he feels he is good
enough to order his own mallet with his ini-
tials on top of the handle.*

—Peter Maas

One of the great qualities of backyard—usually nine-wicket—
croquet is its adaptability. It is best played on a lawn that is
big, flat, smooth, and fast; but it can also be played on one that is
small, sloped, and lumpy. That's convenient because most people
have less-than-perfect lawns.

Figure 1 shows the USCA nine-wicket, two-stake layout with
direction of play. The "official" court is 100 by 50 feet, about one
ninth of an acre. If you live on a quarter-acre lot, it is doubtful
that you will be able to devote almost half your property to a croquet court. No matter. The game will shrink to fit; proportion-
ately reduce the distances between wickets, maintaining a
rectangle with a length-to-width ratio of close to 2:1. (Need to
include a turn in your course? Consider making an L-shaped
court.) It's best if the playing surface is at least 25 by 50 feet.

To set up a nine-wicket course, first drive the two stakes into
the ground at either end of the court, halfway between the sidelines. Then set the two wickets closest to each stake, as near to 6
feet apart as possible. The other five wickets are then placed to
form a course with the shape and dimensions—or at least
ratios—shown in figure 1. Although the "double diamond" is the
official pattern to this course, wide variations are permitted in
the backyard game.

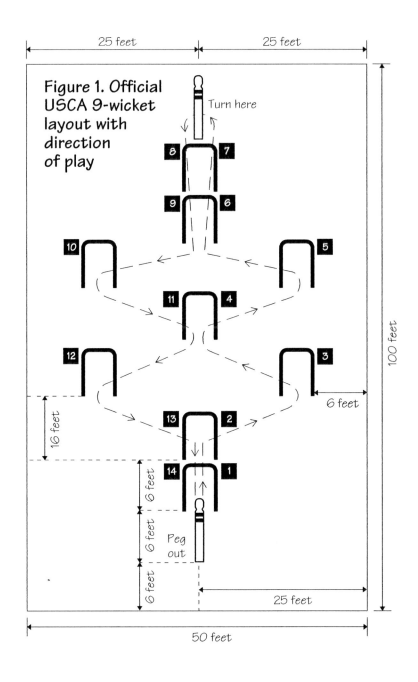

Figure 1. Official USCA 9-wicket layout with direction of play

> **A**s Confucius would say, "The more precise the boundary lines, the fewer the arguments."

Away from American backyards, the rest of the world plays six-wicket croquet. It is a more challenging game and therefore the choice of accomplished players, but to establish a proper course takes an even larger lawn than does the nine-wicket game. The goal is the same for both versions: to race your opponent(s) around a course of wickets and hit the finishing stake before they do.

Figure 2 shows the USCA six-wicket, one-stake layout. Although the official court, 105 by 84 feet, is bigger than many backyards, you can get by with an area of lawn 45 by 36 feet. Simply scale down the distances between wickets and boundaries, maintaining an overall length-width ratio of 5:4.

> **"O**n my course, you have to go through a rubber tire and go round the hammock just to get to the first wicket."
>
> —Jim Bouton

One method is to use units of ten to establish court dimensions. Thus, one possibility is a court 40 feet wide (four units) by 50 feet long (five units) with the stake in the middle at the intersection of the two diagonals. The corner wickets would then be one unit from their adjacent boundaries, and the center wickets one unit in each direction from the stake.

	Official Size	Alternate Size	Alternate Size
Boundary Lines (Ends x Sides)	50' x 100'	40' x 80'	10' x 20'
Distance Between Boundary Lines & Stakes	6'	5'	1'
Distance Between Stakes & Wickets 1+7, 1+2, 6+7	6'	5'	1 1/2'
Distance Between Wickets 3, 5, 10, 12, & Side Boundaries	6'	5'	1 1/2'

USCA nine-wicket, two-stake court variations.

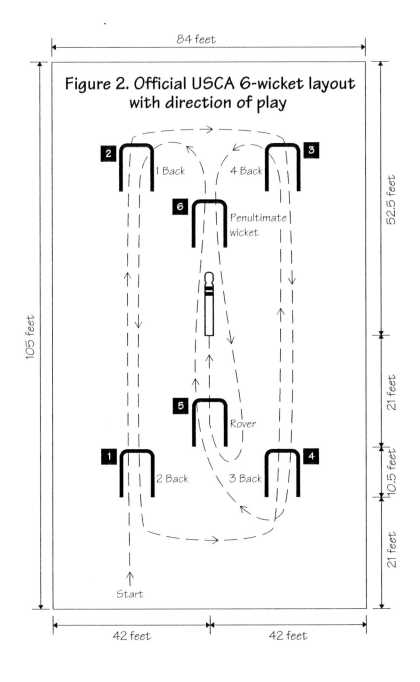

Figure 2. Official USCA 6-wicket layout with direction of play

If your lawn is smaller still, you might try a five-hoop setting. Don't feel that croquet on a smaller court is somehow inadequate. You should find it easier to play breaks, making the game more fun.

LAWNS

Unlike Britain, where climate and soil conditions are fairly constant, lawns in America vary enormously by region. In general, though, if you want to plant a lawn that can double as a croquet court, consider the following suggestions.

1. Rototill the soil.
2. Add lime and fertilizer. Consult your local nursery for advice on how to treat your particular soil.
3. Rake the ground level.
4. Spread seed at a rate of at least three to four pounds per 1,000 square feet. Overseed the first couple of years. Consider using creeping bentgrass, which provides a good playing surface.
5. Maintaining your lawn may necessitate one or more of the following:

- Installing a peripheral or portable watering system. Avoid sprinkler heads on the court that make your ball go bumpity-bump.
- Buying a good lawn mower with adjustable blades. Croquet can be played on grass with weeds and bare spots, and it even can be played on sloping lawns dotted with trees, but the game suffers greatly when played on long grass. Strikers are forced to swing too hard, at the cost of accuracy, and they tend to swing down on the ball,

All Measurements are Shown Ends x Sides	Official Size	Alternate Size	Half Size	Alternate Size	Alternate Size
Boundary Lines	84' x 105'	60' x 74'	42' x 52 $\frac{1}{2}$'	30' x 37'	21' x 26 $\frac{1}{4}$'
Distance From Corner Wickets to Boundary Lines	21' x 21'	15' x 15'	10 $\frac{1}{2}$' x 10 $\frac{1}{2}$'	7 $\frac{1}{2}$' x 7 $\frac{1}{2}$'	5 $\frac{1}{4}$' x5 $\frac{1}{4}$'
Distance From Boundary lines to Center stake	42' x 52 $\frac{1}{2}$'	30' x 37'	26' x 21'	15' x 18 $\frac{1}{2}$'	13' x 10 $\frac{1}{2}$'
Distance From Stake to Infield Wickets	21'	15'	10 $\frac{1}{2}$'	7 $\frac{1}{2}$'	5 $\frac{1}{2}$'

USCA six-wicket, one-stake court variations.

causing it to jump. Certain shots can't be practiced, much less perfected.

The court should be mowed often, rolled infrequently. Too much rolling compacts the soil and inhibits growth. For backyard croquet, a grass height of a quarter-inch is sufficient. At croquet clubs, mower blades are often set to cut half that length, but that is probably unwise unless you have a gardener in the house.

Keep in mind that the ideal croquet lawn is not the rich green hue that we have come to love. If you want to develop touch in croquet, the court should be fast and slightly straw-colored.

- Fertilizing and pest control, including the elimination of weeds, fungus, and insects. Garden centers have many different chemicals to attack those problems.

"**A**lice thought she had never seen such a curious croquet-ground in her life: it was all ridges and furrows; the balls were live hedgehogs, and the mallets live flamingos, and the soldiers had to double themselves up and stand on their hands and feet to make the arches."
                    —**Lewis Carroll,** *Alice in Wonderland*

EQUIPMENT

There is as great a gap between backyard and championship croquet equipment as between baseball and whiffleball equipment. Backyard sets can be purchased at most large sporting-goods stores. Forster Inc. in Wilton, Maine, is the popular choice for backyard equipment. Starter sets include six mallets and balls, nine wickets, and two stakes. The mallets are made of hardwood, the balls are three inches in diameter, and the wickets are wide and hospitable.

Move up to club croquet and you get to play with bigger balls, bigger mallets, and narrower hoops.

Mallet

This is the only piece of croquet equipment that players can choose and personalize. Players have been known to inscribe their name—or their mallet's name—on the head or shaft, but most dismiss that as too brazen. "I call my mallet 'The Terminator,'" says Wayne Rodoni, "but I would never actually put that on the mallet."

Since it's the most important piece of equipment in the game, anyone purchasing an individual mallet should try out as many as possible. Borrow before you buy.

There is a wide price range, from $30 for an entire garden set to custom-made mallets for $400. In the past, serious players generally ordered their equipment from John Jaques of Surrey, England. Today, many serious players order their mallets from Bob Jackson of New Zealand.

The story is told of the American tourist in England who admired a lawn at a Cambridge college. "How do you achieve that beautiful surface?" the tourist asked the gardener.

"Simple, sir," replied the gardener. "Just mow it and roll it, mow it and roll it—every day for two hundred years."

Mallets legally can be any weight or length, though most good ones weigh three pounds and have a three-foot shaft. Backyard mallets are closer to two feet long and weigh much less. The two mallet faces can be any shape, but they must be identical, parallel, and perpendicular to the bottom of the head. Mallet faces can be coated with anything that doesn't offer an advantage over wood. Backyard mallets have plastic impact caps on the face. Many top-flight players opt for Delrin, a plastic coating that prevents the wooden face from breaking down.

The heads may be either round or square, and though backyard mallets are always round, many top players prefer square heads. The biggest advantage of a square-headed mallet is that it will stand on its own. Although it won't make you a better player, it's pretty handy when you want to mark where a ball went out of bounds.

Mallet care. Regardless of the quality of your mallet, you must protect it from prolonged exposure to rain or dampness. Dry and clean it after each use. Apply an occasional coat of furniture polish to wooden surfaces. Store it in a cool, dry place, ideally upside down between two pegs. Don't stand a mallet in a corner, as that can warp the shaft. Hit only the croquet balls appropriate for that mallet. With proper use and care, a good mallet can last a lifetime.

Balls

Most backyard balls are three inches in diameter. Association, or club, balls are bigger (about $3\,{}^5/_8$ inches) and heavier (about sixteen ounces). Most have a composition core with a plastic cover.

Consider buying larger tournament balls to improve your game. The extra weight of the bigger balls allows them to travel more smoothly over an imperfect surface. This permits you to develop a wider range of shots.

Wickets

The biggest difference between backyard sets and club sets is perhaps wicket size. Less expensive backyard croquet sets feature rounded, flexible wire hoops, which can be bent into a variety of widths to accommodate less precise shooting.

Official wickets are made of rounded iron that will not easily bend to shape. The crown is straight and at right angles to the uprights. The distance between the uprights, uniform for the entire wicket, should be between $3\,{}^{11}/_{16}$ and 4 inches. This leaves a clearance between ball and official wicket of only $^1/_{16}$ to $^3/_8$ of an inch.

Stakes

Backyard stakes are wooden dowels with colored bands that, reading from top to bottom—blue, red, black, and yellow—indicate order of play. [That could be helpful after the fifth Mai Tai.]

STANCE, GRIP, AND SWING

....

*The chief difficulty Alice found at first was
managing her flamingo; she succeeded in
getting its body tucked away, comfortable
enough, under her arm, with its legs hanging down, but generally, just as she had got
its neck nicely straightened out, and was
going to give the hedgehog a blow with its
head, it would twist itself around and look
up at her, with such a puzzled expression
that she could not help bursting out laugh-
ing. . . . Alice came to the conclusion that it
was a very difficult game indeed.*

—Lewis Carroll,
Alice in Wonderland

Before you can become an able shot-maker, you must decide
where to stand in relation to the ball, how to grip the mallet,
and what constitutes a good swing. The key to good croquet is
feeling comfortable over the ball.

The only way to find your personal comfort zone is to spend
time trying all the different grips and stances. Shuffle your feet
around; move your hands up and down the shaft. Think of the
croquet mallet as your bag of clubs. Faced with a 100-yard golf
shot, you would probably pull out a wedge; a 180-yard shot might
call for a 4-iron. But in croquet, you have only one mallet, and it's
the position of your hands and feet that determines whether you
hit a stop shot, a pass roll, or something in between.

Once you find each shot on your club, practice it until you are
comfortable with it. "Then," says Rhys Thomas, "you are pre-
pared to play a really nice game."

STANCE

There are two croquet stances for the serious player: *side* and *center* styles.

If you ask complete novices to hit a croquet ball, odds are they will assume a golf stance, in which they swing the mallet at a right angle to the direction they are facing. If they have played golf or baseball, novice strikers seem most comfortable in this position. But a golf stance is ineffective in croquet. It allows the striker to hit the ball hard, but pinpoint accuracy is impossible because the striker can't sight over the ball to the target. No top-flight croquet players use a golf stance. You shouldn't use one either—except perhaps to hit a long shot on a thick lawn.

Side style

In the side style, the mallet is swung outside the body and parallel to the feet. Like the golf stance, the side style originated in an era when women wore long, billowy dresses that prevented their swinging a mallet between their legs. It offers some of the power of the golf stance and some of the control of the center style.

The side style and the golf stance have something else in common: They don't allow the striker to eyeball the shot from directly over the ball. Strikers can compensate by moving their head over the line of the swing. In this way, their body weight is supported by the foot nearest the mallet while the other foot is used mostly for balance.

The biggest advantage of the side style is that it allows a free backswing, enabling those with weaker arms and wrists to generate power with a bigger swing.

Center style

The center style (fig. 3) allows strikers to face the target and swing the mallet pendulum-style between their legs. The advantage is that strikers stand behind the ball and swing directly through the line of aim.

The knees should be slightly bent, the feet quite close together. Good players tend to spread them less than a foot apart,

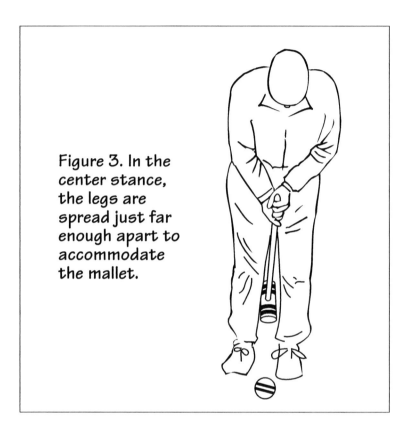

Figure 3. In the center stance, the legs are spread just far enough apart to accommodate the mallet.

leaving just enough room for the swinging mallet. Most strikers "square off" to their target—that is, both feet are equally far forward, weight evenly balanced.

But John Solomon, who many claim is the best croquet player who ever lived, believes the striker should move one foot forward until the toe of the back foot is about even with the heel of the front foot. If you are right-handed (your right hand is the lower hand in your grip), then move the right foot back. This permits a freer backswing before your hand hits your leg.

In this position, Solomon says, "your body need no longer be rigid but can be free to follow, in a small degree, the movement of the mallet. You are now able to rock backwards and forward on your feet, and this means that your whole stroke will become more relaxed, more supple and, what is of great importance, less tiring."

The big advantage of the center style is that the mallet is swung along the aim line, which naturally tends to be straight. Ensuring a straight swing with the side style is a bit harder.

In the 1994 World Croquet Championship, all twenty-eight players used the center style. Even if you are a beginner, it makes sense to mimic those who are successful.

If you become semiserious about croquet, you will adopt either the side or center style. Which one you choose will depend on how comfortable you feel and how successful you are. Experiment with both. You might try the side style for power strokes and the center style for running hoops.

A croquet stance is largely a matter of individual preference. Move your feet around until you find the one best suited for your game.

Whichever stance you choose, your ultimate goal is to move beyond thought, to a point where foot placement, grip, and swing are instinctive and automatic.

GRIP

Watch good players and you will soon spot the three most common grips: *standard*, *Irish*, and *Solomon*.

Standard grip

In the standard grip (fig. 4), also called the *reverse-palm grip,* the knuckles of the upper hand and the palm of the lower hand face forward.

Grasp the top of the mallet with your left hand (if you are left-handed, reverse this), curling your fingers around the shaft and pointing your knuckles toward the target. No part of the hand should be covering the very top of the shaft. Place your right hand just below the left, fingers down, palm facing the target. Grip tightly with the left hand, more lightly with the right hand, which is used mainly for balance.

In what some refer to as the American version of this grip (fig. 5), the hands are well separated, with the right hand six to twelve inches below the left, palm facing forward, and index finger

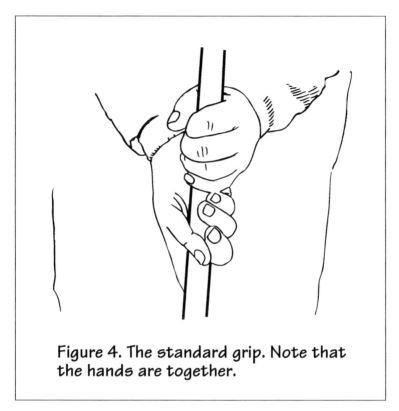

Figure 4. The standard grip. Note that
the hands are together.

pointing down along the side or the back of the mallet shaft.

In the "pencil-grip" variation of this grip, the right hand cups the handle between the thumb and forefinger, with the middle finger down the side and the fourth finger against the back.

Irish grip

Although you would be wise to abandon the golf stance, you may find that something approaching a golf grip works in croquet. This is called the Irish grip (fig. 6), originated by the great Irish players around the turn of the century. This grip has both palms facing away from the body and the fingers pointing downward. The lower hand often encloses the thumb or fingers of the upper hand, much the same way most golfers hold a golf club.

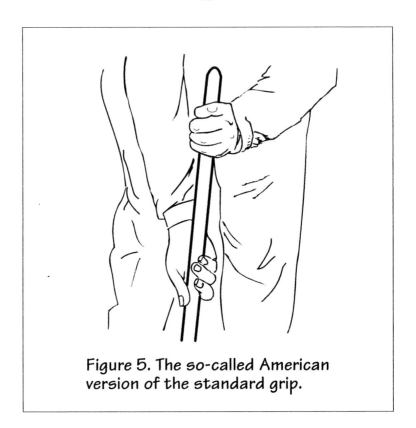

Figure 5. The so-called American version of the standard grip.

Solomon grip

John Solomon, dissatisfied with both of the established grips, adopted a third that was named for him. In the Solomon grip (fig. 7), the knuckles of both hands point forward with the thumbs behind. "I used not to encourage people to play with this grip," says Solomon, "but I have since come to the conclusion that it is my grip which has given me any success I may have had. I believe the reason to be that, each hand being held in the same position, each works in a complimentary way to the other. Neither hand has any predominance and the result is a perfect blend between the two."

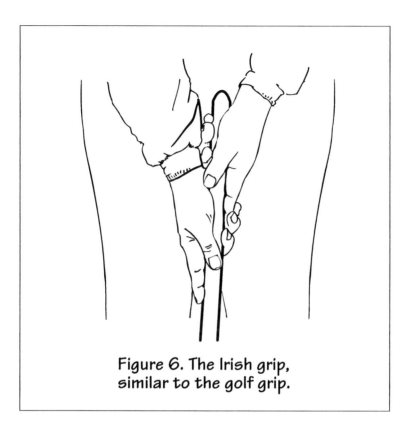

**Figure 6. The Irish grip,
similar to the golf grip.**

STALK AND SWING

Before you can swing, you must first line up the shot. Even in practice, stalk each shot carefully. Stand well behind your ball and sight over it toward your target. Square your shoulders and feet. Adjust your position until you are right on target. Approach the ball along the imaginary line that you have set.

Like golfers, croquet players address the ball before each shot. Except in the case of the few players who favor a perpetual-motion style, the striker's mallet during this phase should rest gently on the grass, the center of its face a half-inch or so behind the center of the ball.

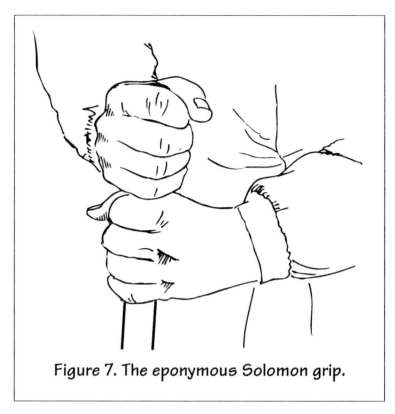

Figure 7. The eponymous Solomon grip.

Point your feet—and thus square your shoulders—to your target. Relax and bend your knees. Train your eyes on the spot of lawn just behind your ball, where the mallet will reach the bottom of its arc and lightly brush the grass surface. After you have addressed the ball, take a final look at the target. If you feel you have lined up the shot improperly, back off and start over. Don't just shuffle your feet around on the spot.

Strive for a loose, natural, straight swing. Imagine a pendulum swinging freely back and forth, back and forth. Start the swing from the shoulders, not from the elbows, letting your arms and mallet move as one. Try to take your wrists out of the swing, at least until you're proficient. The rest of your body should remain still during the swing. The backswing, like the forward swing, should be steady and unhurried. How far back you take the mallet depends on how hard you intend to hit the shot.

"**I** have tried it [the Irish grip] on a number of occasions but find it difficult to get any control at all, and a great strain also on the backswing—in fact, I have never been able to understand how anybody ever managed to do anything when playing with the Irish grip."

—**John Solomon**

Keep the head down and swing through the line that you established when you stalked the shot. Don't straighten up until after the ball has left your field of vision. Continue to look at the grass below the departed ball as you finish with a complete follow-through, pushing your arms away from your body, "carrying the mallet through," as croquet author Lord Tollemache wrote. One instructor tells his students to "imagine you are trying to hit the underside of a bucket hanging in front of you about three feet off the ground." The swing should end with the arms extended but not stiff. Look up only after you have completely finished your swing.

Now that you have all that information percolating through your brain, try to relax and forget it. If you are deep in analysis of your swing, it means you are not relaxed, which is the key to being a successful croquet player. Of course, you can't relax and rely on instinct until you develop some. To accomplish that, you must practice extensively to ingrain the various shots in muscle memory.

John Solomon has likened playing croquet to listening to music: "You can listen to every note and establish its position within the framework of the whole piece, or you can detach yourself from it, letting the music put you in an emotional frame of mind outside yourself. A croquet swing should be like that: a movement of the arms that is unconsciously performed and results in a perfect swing."

HITTING A CROQUET BALL

. . . .

You can learn to hit the ball very easily,
but to learn the strategy takes a minimum
of two years.

—Darryl Zanuck

ONE-BALL SHOTS

The-first skill you need to practice and improve is hitting your
own ball with accuracy. After all, the first stroke of every turn is
a one-ball shot, as are most shots that run wickets. The final shot
of the game—the *stake-out*—is usually a one-ball shot. Strikers
who can consistently hit their own ball where they want will be
nearly unbeatable.

The basic single-ball shots are *running wickets* and *roquets*.

Running wickets—straight shot

Place your ball a few feet directly in front of a wicket. Stand two
or three yards behind the ball and sight through the center of the
ball to the center of the wicket. The two centers and your sighting
eye should be on one line. See that line in your mind's eye. Take a
mental photograph.

Hold that line as you walk toward your ball. This is called
stalking. When you reach your ball, assume a comfortable stance
and address the ball (fig. 8). If you have stalked the ball correctly
and use the center stance, your feet will be properly aligned. As
your feet go, so goes your swing.

Take another look at the target, the center of the hoop. If
your alignment seems off, go back and stalk again. Don't just
shuffle your feet on the spot to try to achieve proper alignment.

Once you are set, take a deep breath and exhale. Stay loose.

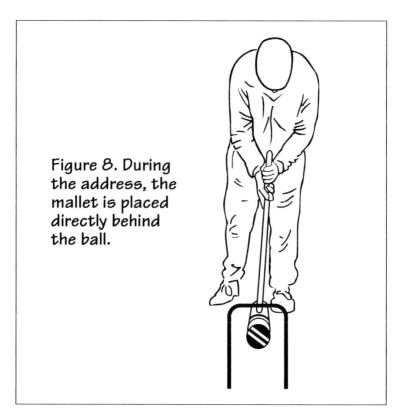

Figure 8. During the address, the mallet is placed directly behind the ball.

Faced with a long roquet or a sticky wicket, most people tend to tighten their muscles. That's a bad move. Instead, relax. Shake out your arm and leg muscles, loosen your grip, and take slow, deep breaths.

Take a slow, steady backswing and a fluid forward swing. Don't rush anything; let the mallet head do its thing. Carry the mallet head through, pushing your arms away from your body (fig. 9). A good follow-through puts forward spin on the ball (as a pool player does by hitting the cue ball slightly above center). Visualize the mallet head following the ball through the wicket. Avoid jabbing with the mallet, as that will make the ball skid along the ground for the first few inches before it begins to roll. When that happens, the ball often lacks the spin necessary to pull it through a wicket.

You've aimed for the center of the wicket—now forget it. Focus on a piece of grass just beyond the hoop.

Determine where you want your ball to stop, and swing no harder than necessary. The advantage of a hard hit is that on a slightly bumpy court, the ball will not be diverted by minor imperfections. On very bumpy courts, however, a hard hit may bounce over the target. In general, it is best to hit smooth and straight, and as gently as you can. A ball struck gently will roll—not skid—from the outset.

Your head should stay down, eyes locked on the spot the ball left, until you have finished the follow-through.

Now repeat the above sequence dozens of times.

Figure 9. The aftermath of the shot. Note the complete follow-through, the arms pushed well away from the body.

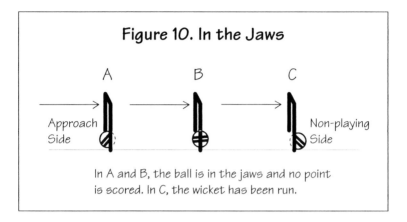

Figure 10. In the Jaws

A   B   C

Approach   Non-playing
Side   Side

In A and B, the ball is in the jaws and no point
is scored. In C, the wicket has been run.

Running wickets—angle shots

Do all of the above, plus the following:
- Walk around behind the wicket and sight back toward the ball. If you don't have an unobstructed view of the ball, you can't run the wicket. If that's the case, consider playing for position.
- If you do have a shot, aim to brush the inside edge of the near upright. It's possible that the far side of your ball will nudge the inside of the far upright, but if you play the shot with follow-through (thereby imparting spin), the ball has a chance to run the wicket.
- Try this exercise: Place balls eighteen inches in front of a wicket, thirty degrees off line—at about five o'clock and seven o'clock—and practice running the wicket. Count the shot as successful only if the ball finishes at least two feet clear of the other side of the wicket. Once you have mastered this shot, widen the angle slightly and practice from there. Determine the widest angle from which wickets can be run.

Roquets

Beginners can become obsessed with trying to run wickets, at the expense of the roquet shot. Yet the roquet—hitting your ball into another ball upon which you are alive—is the only way to earn two extra shots. Your only chance to run a series of wickets (make a *break*) is to make heavy use of the roquet.

When learning any new skill, stay with the basics. Line up each shot. Draw an imaginary line. Photograph it. Align your feet. Now approach your ball along that line. When you reach your ball, hold your mallet above the line and recheck your alignment and aim. Does the sight line on top of the mallet match your imaginary line? If not, back off and restalk. If it looks good, lower your eyes and mallet to the ball.

"**The great secret of rushing is to imagine you are actually going to drive the *other* ball with your mallet. You should actually regard your own ball as part of the head of the mallet, which is going to brush and sweep the other ball along.**"
—**Lord Tollemache**

Take a slow backswing and a smooth, even forward swing. Hit through the center of the ball, making contact at the bottom of the swing, the mallet parallel to the ground. Keep your head down, looking up only after the ball is well on its way toward the target.

Practice roquets at close range. At first, just try hitting your ball into a target ball. When you have gained confidence from three feet away, try extending the distance to four feet, and so on.

If—when—you regress to where you are again missing short roquets, you have probably strayed from the basics. The two most common mistakes are a misaligned stance and a moving head.

Rush

Let's say that once in a while, you're able to smash your ball into another ball from a pretty fair distance. Now it's time to work on control.

The *rush* is a roquet in which you hit your ball into another ball, sending the roqueted ball to a predetermined spot, or at

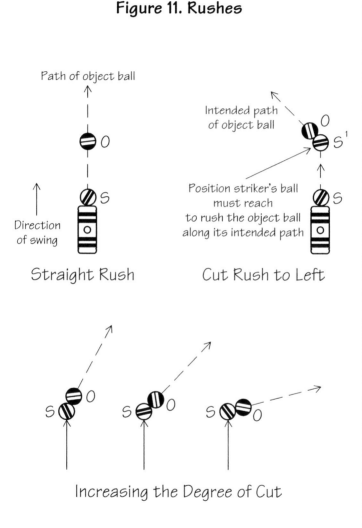

Figure 11. Rushes

Path of object ball

O

S

Direction
of swing

Straight Rush

Intended path
of object ball

O

S¹

S

Position striker's ball
must reach
to rush the object ball
along its intended path

Cut Rush to Left

S O

S O

S O

Increasing the Degree of Cut

least in a predetermined direction. *Straight rushes* send both balls directly forward in a straight line.

You should concentrate on direction at first, gradually increasing the distance between the two balls and the strength of your rushes. Clarify your goals before each swing. Be clear on where you want both balls to stop. Be honest about your results. Practice. Experiment.

Work for precision. Beginners tend to be satisfied if their ball stops in the neighborhood of a wicket. But the *cognoscenti* know that the ideal rush will position the roqueted ball about three feet in front of the wicket and no more than a foot off center.

Cut rush

Suppose you don't want to send both balls straight ahead, but wish to send them at divergent angles. You need a *cut rush*.

The principle here is the same as in pool or billiards. If you want to cut-rush an object ball to the right, you must aim your striker's ball to hit the left side of the object ball. To move it left, aim to hit the right side of the object ball. To hit it to the extreme right or left, increase the degree of cut.

As you practice, pay close attention to the angles described by the balls in your roquets. Learn from your *leaves*.

One caveat: You should attempt cut rushes only when the gap between striker's ball and object ball is a couple of feet or less. If the gap is much larger than that, you risk missing altogether. That "safe" distance will vary with court quality and skill level.

Experiment with the power variable. The more cut required, the more power required to move the object ball an equal distance. That's because the striker's ball hits farther from the object ball's center, thereby transmitting less energy to the object ball; in contrast, a straight rush transfers nearly a full load of energy to the object ball, and so the object ball rolls and the striker's ball stops quickly.

Remember that with rush shots, you are concerned only with where the object ball stops. The final resting place of the striker's ball is inconsequential, for after a roquet, the striker picks up his or her ball (ball-in-hand) to take croquet. Focus on guiding the roqueted ball to the desired spot.

It's not uncommon for beginners to hit a bouncer that hops

over the object ball. Sometimes you can blame a bumpy lawn. If that's your problem, practice your rushes on a relatively smooth part of it. You can't improve if success is totally random.

A lot of successful croquet players are scientists, mathematicians, computer programmers, or at least people who can apply basic principles of geometry and physics.

A bouncer can also be caused by what is sometimes called the "magnet effect." This is when the striker, drawn irresistibly to the object ball, leans forward, placing weight on the front part of the feet and inadvertently tilting the mallet face downward. From this position, the striker will hit the ball slightly into the turf, which can cause it to rebound into the air. Solution: After stalking the shot and determining the aim line, concentrate on keeping your head down, weight evenly distributed, body still. Move only your arms in a smooth, pendulumlike swing. Avoid jerky movements.

Practice cut-rushing balls to a target a few feet away. Start with shots that require only a slight cut left or right. As you improve, increase the distance and degree of cut.

Rhys Thomas spoke to me about how the rule differences between the American and international games hurt American players:

"One of the differences in the American rules versus the international rules is that we Americans have deadness. If you hit a ball, you're dead on it until you run a wicket. The result is that American players are afraid to hit balls and become dead. In international rules, players hit balls all the time. Consequently, their croquet shots are a lot better than ours. It's essential to practice the croquet stroke when the croquet stroke is called for.

"Beginners in backyard croquet think that the cruelest thing you can do is to put your foot on your ball and smash the opponent into oblivion. But running wickets by using croquet strokes is much crueler. We use the opponent ball, not once but repeatedly. Then when we're done, we cast it aside like an olive pit."

TWO-BALL (CROQUET) SHOTS

You know now that a roquet earns the striker two bonus strokes, the first of which should be a croquet shot. To take croquet, the striker picks up his or her ball and carries it to where the roqueted ball has stopped. The striker's ball is then placed anywhere next to and touching the roqueted ball.

You can only control the balls in a croquet shot if they are touching. But often when you place your ball next to the target ball, they move apart.
To assure contact, press your thumb into the grass under the near lip of the target ball and place your ball in that imprint. Check to make sure that your ball is in that imprint and that both balls are touching.

The focus of the croquet shot should be control of both balls. Players should put aside youthful machismo, a mind-set that elevated the foot shot to high art. If you want to advance your croquet game, you must try to position both balls so that they help you make breaks.

The basic two-ball shots are the *drive, roll* (full, half, pass), *split shot, stop shot, peel,* and *cannon.*

Drive

The drive, in which both balls travel in the same direction, is the most basic croquet shot, making it a logical starting point for beginners.

Place the striker's ball behind the ball to be croqueted so that the centers line up with the target. Place the mallet head behind both centers, and aim along that target line.

Play the stroke as if the second ball were not there, remembering to follow through. The drive is the only two-ball shot in which you hit the ball squarely, at the bottom of the swing pendulum. Have someone else check that your mallet head is parallel to the ground on impact.

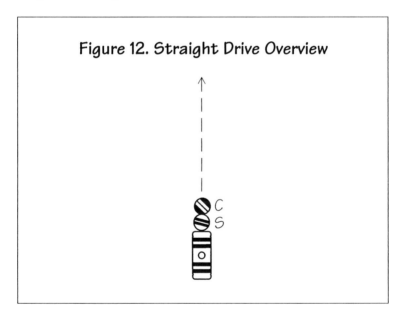

Figure 12. Straight Drive Overview

A smooth, square hit will send the average croqueted ball three times as far as the striker's ball (fig. 13). Experience will help you determine your own personal ratio, which may be different. Knowing your own ratio will help you figure out whether your striker's ball should travel farther (tending toward a full roll) or shorter (tending toward a stop shot).

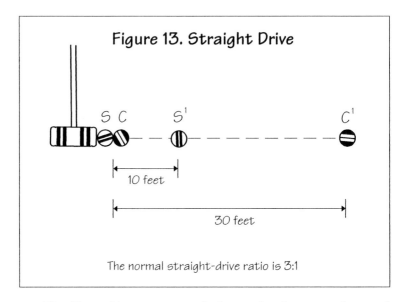

Figure 13. Straight Drive

S C   S¹   C¹

|← 10 feet →|

|←   30 feet   →|

The normal straight-drive ratio is 3:1

Tip. To avoid two common faults, maintain an evenly paced swing to the completion of the follow-through. If you accelerate the swing after your mallet makes contact with the ball, you risk *pushing* or *shepherding* the ball. If the mallet head remains in contact with the striker's ball after the croqueted ball loses contact with it, it's a fault. If you slow your swing during follow-through, you risk a *double tap,* another fault.

Practice. Set down a target about thirty feet away and play some straight drives, trying to stop the croqueted ball near the target. Measure how far the object ball travels compared to the striker's ball. Are you near a 3:1 ratio? As you improve, move the targets farther away. If it makes you practice more often, keep score or make the exercise competitive. Closest ball to the target wins.

Roll

By manipulating your stance, grip, and mallet-head angle, you can affect different spins on the striker's ball, thus changing the distance it travels. If you are an experienced spin-master, you can achieve ratios from 2:1 (*half roll:* striker's ball travels half as far as object ball) to less than 1:1 (*pass roll:* striker's ball travels farther than the croqueted ball).

Full roll. To achieve a full roll in which the striker's ball travels about the same distance as the croqueted ball, try the following (reverse your hands and feet if you are left-handed):

- Stand closer to the balls than you would for a drive. Your left foot should be forward, about four inches to the side of the two balls. This foot should be flat on the ground, bearing most of your body weight. Your right foot should be twelve to fifteen inches behind the striker's ball and slightly to the left of a line running through the centers of the balls. Use your right foot to balance, keeping only your toes on the ground. Bend both knees sharply until you reach what could be called a "crouched side style."
- Your left hand should be about a quarter of the way down the shaft; your right hand about three quarters of the way down. The knuckles of your upper hand and the palm of your lower hand should face forward.
- Incline the mallet so that its shaft angles forward and its toe points downward.
- Take a relatively short backswing and hit down on the striker's ball, contacting it above center.
- Follow through.

Half roll. This stroke can be played center style, with the striker's ball lying just between your two big toes. Hold the mallet about a third of the way down the shaft and hit just above the center of the striker's ball (lower than for a full roll). Use a chopping motion, with minimal follow-through.

Practice. As you hit rolls, experiment with grip and stance. Tiny adjustments will alter the spin on the striker's ball, and hence the ratio achieved. Adjust the angle of the mallet face and the impact point of mallet on ball. Store the results in an active file in your muscle memory.

Pass roll. This shot, when executed properly, will send the

1

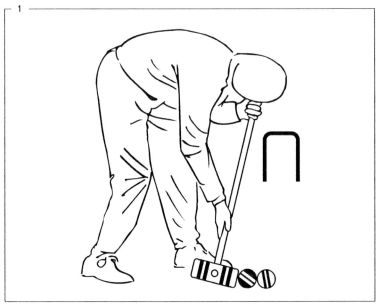

2

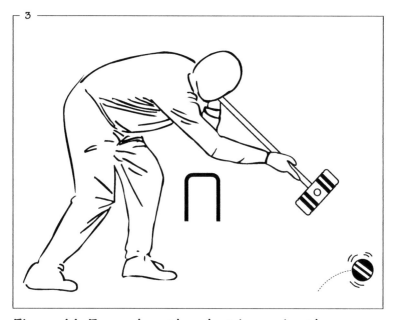

Figure 14. Even when the shot is easier than this pass roll, stay with the basics and don't skip steps. For each swing, pay attention to hand placement, stance, body position, swing, follow-through.

striker's ball farther than the croqueted ball. Most croquet players give the roll shots a high degree of difficulty. Says Rhys Thomas: "If you don't have a full roll and a pass roll, you will lose. When I was beginning, I would go out and hit two to three hundred full rolls a day, every day for six months. I vowed I would never lose a game because of a full roll or pass roll."

Whether you are going to hit two or two thousand, try to do them right. If you are right-handed, place your left foot next to the striker's ball and your right foot well back, with your head, hands, and body weight directly over the ball. Try to find a comfort zone in this deep crouch. Take a short backswing, keeping your weight forward, and hit sharply down, aiming for the top third of the ball. Carry the mallet through. The ball should jump a little, overtake, and pass the croqueted ball on a slightly divergent line. "You have to find where you are comfortable," says Thomas. "The only way to do that is to keep doing it."

Tip. The shaft of the mallet should tilt even farther forward than for a full roll. Thus, you will have to lean unnaturally forward, with your back close to horizontal.

Split shot

A split shot is a croquet shot that sends the two balls on divergent paths. It is hit with the mallet head parallel to the ground— that is, with no element of roll or stop.

Experience will teach you how hard to swing. Figure 15 will teach you about angle of swing.

The upper half of figure 15 illustrates a stroke played with a twenty-degree angle of swing. Note that the angle is measured from the line of centers to the line the mallet travels, and that the striker's ball has traveled a third line.

The lower half of the figure shows a stroke played with a forty-five-degree angle of swing. Note that the balls have diverged at an angle of ninety degrees (the maximum possible in a legal croquet stroke) and that they have traveled equal distances.

Increasing the angle of swing above forty-five degrees does not change the direction the balls travel, only the distance they travel.

When you put your ball in contact with another ball, an imaginary line through the two centers indicates the direction in which the croqueted ball will go. The line your ball will take forms the second leg of a V, the vertex of which is the striker's ball. Your swing line should bisect that V.

Hit shot after shot, working on distance and angle, until you believe the following truths:

- The croqueted ball will always travel the line of centers of the two balls.
- As you increase the angle of swing, the striker's ball travels farther, the croqueted ball less far.
- The striker's ball does not travel in the direction of the mallet swing, except as the angle nears ninety degrees.

Figure 15. Split Shot

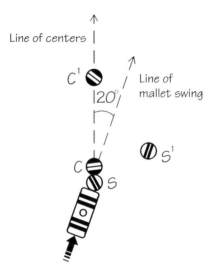

Line of centers

C^1

120°

Line of
mallet swing

S^1

C

S

20° Angle of Swing

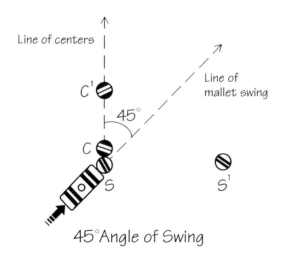

Line of centers

Line of
mallet swing

C^1

45°

C

S

S^1

45° Angle of Swing

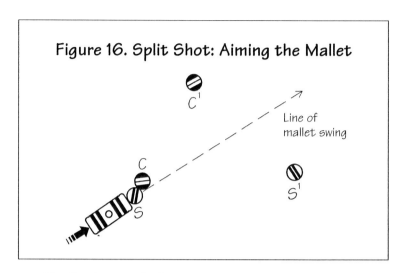

Figure 16. Split Shot: Aiming the Mallet

Tip. Don't try to do the impossible. For example, it is not possible, in a legal croquet shot where both balls must move, to have the balls diverge at an angle greater than ninety degrees. If you play a croquet shot with an angle greater than ninety degrees—that is, you are playing away from the croqueted ball—the croqueted ball will not even shake. That's a fault, and the end of your turn.

Practice. Put up wickets and stakes at different angles, and create different challenges to hold your interest. Measure and mark thirty, forty, sixty, and ninety degrees to give your practice sessions meaning. Try a range of split shots of varying angles. Have a purpose with each shot. Visualize where on the court you want the balls to stop, and honestly appraise your leaves.

Take-off. A *take-off* is a type of split shot played with an angle of swing approaching ninety degrees (fig. 17). This means the striker's ball travels much farther than the croqueted ball. In figure 17, the croqueted ball has barely moved (it need only shake), while the striker's ball has traveled a long way.

When the angle of swing exceeds eighty degrees, the shot is played with only one goal in mind—to direct the striker's ball to a specific spot on the court.

As the angle of swing approaches ninety degrees (a thin take-off), the risk increases that the striker won't move the croqueted ball at all. It's even more likely on bumpy surfaces, where it's hard to position the striker's ball so that it stays in touch with the other ball. If that's your problem, remember to press a thumb into the turf to create a slight depression in which the striker's ball can sit.

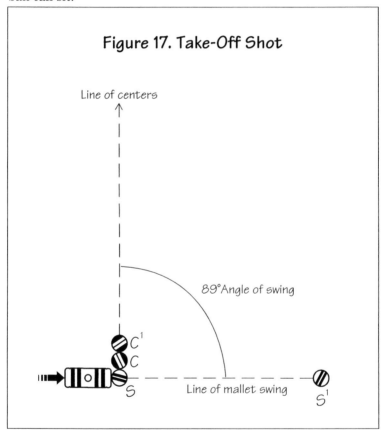

Figure 17. Take-Off Shot

Line of centers

89°Angle of swing

C^1

C

S

Line of mallet swing

S^1

Now that you have two balls side by side, check your aim by placing the mallet head flush with both balls. The handle should point toward your target. To assure that the croqueted ball shakes, aim slightly in its direction. Slight deflection of the striker's ball off the croqueted ball should direct it toward the target, or thereabouts. Work on it.

Figure 18. Take-Offs

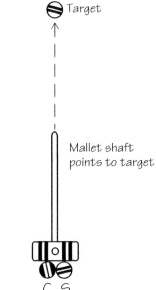

Target

Mallet shaft
points to target

C S

Thin take-off: aiming the striker's ball

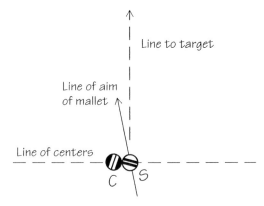

Line to target

Line of aim
of mallet

Line of centers

C S

Tip. The take-off shot is an exception to the rule that strikers should watch only their ball when shooting. Since strikers double as referees, they must keep at least one eye on the croqueted ball to make sure it does something. Although it must shake or rattle, it's under no obligation to roll.

Practice. As always, set up a series of shots of increasing difficulty. Learn what the slight deflection inherent in this shot means for the distance and direction of the striker's ball. Try to put the striker's ball right where you want it. Set up targets to make sure you're not fooling yourself.

Stop shot

The point of the stop shot is to move your ball very little while moving the target ball much farther. If stroked correctly, the target ball will travel up to ten times as far as the striker's ball.

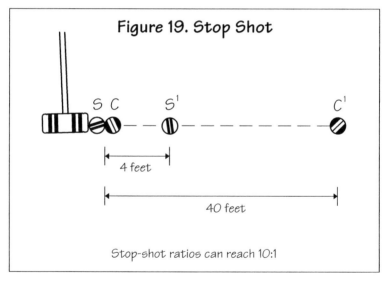

Figure 19. Stop Shot

S C   S^1 C^1

4 feet

40 feet

Stop-shot ratios can reach 10:1

In pool, a player can stop or back up a cue ball by hitting below its center. Croquet mallet faces are too large to permit that, but a similar effect can be achieved by doing the following:

- Take a normal stance, as if you are about to hit a straight drive.

- Take a half step back, but continue holding the mallet face next to the striker's ball. This should tilt the shaft back toward your body. With the heel of the mallet resting on the lawn, the toe should be raised slightly so that the bottom of the hitting face is aimed just below the center of the ball.
- Do not follow through but rather stab at the ball. Some instructors advise grounding the heel of the mallet into the turf just as the striker's ball is hit.

Tip. Unlike many croquet shots, the stop shot does not require a smooth, even swing but rather a poking action. A common mistake is grounding the mallet too far behind the striker's ball, which could make you miss the ball.

Practice. The stop shot requires considerable practice. Start by hitting soft stop shots, in which the croqueted ball travels only a short distance. Estimate where you want to ground the heel of the mallet. Get a feel for the grounding action before you add power.

If you are in England and someone hits a long, well-placed stop shot, it's appropriate to shout, "Good show! Quite a beefy stop shot!"

Persevere, for there will be plenty of chances to hit stop shots. With practice, you will be able to play a stop shot that sends the croqueted ball the length of the court. When that happens, listen carefully for *Ooohs* and *Aaahs* from the other players.

Peel

Named after Walter Peel, nineteenth-century croquet champion and co-founder of England's Croquet Association, this shot separates good players from great players. A peel occurs when you cause a ball other than your own to run a wicket. In most cases, the peeled ball will be your partner ball (singles) or partner's ball (doubles). A peel might be called for when another ball is in the jaws of a wicket or is dead on several balls. By peeling your part-

Figure 20

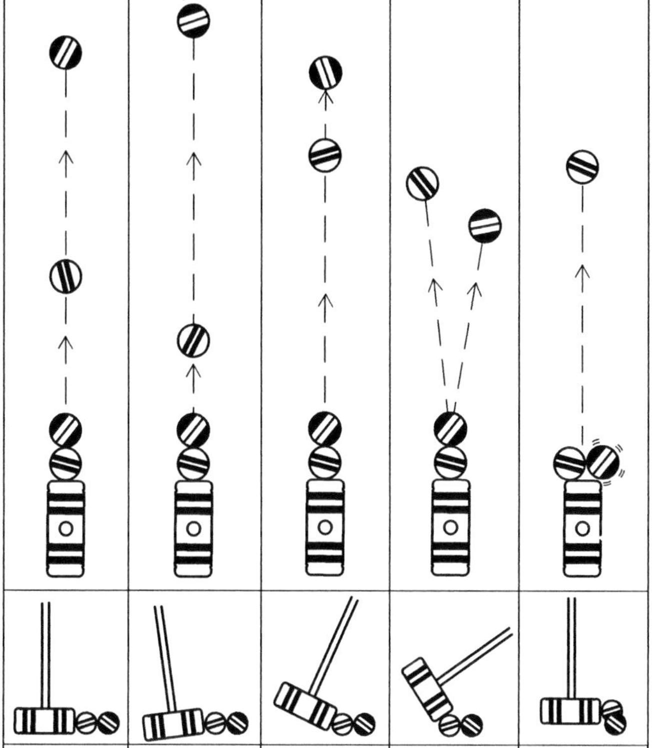

	Drive	Stop Shot	Roll	Pass Roll	Take Off
Stance	Erect, knees flexed	Erect	Crouched, knees bent	Deep crouch	Erect
Hands	Near top of shaft	At top of shaft	At least halfway down shaft	Close to bottom of shaft	Near top of shaft
Feet	Normal	Half a step back from normal	Front foot by side of balls	Front foot by side of balls	Normal
Mallet head	Parallel to ground	Parallel to ground or toe inclined up	Heel of mallet raised	Heel of mallet raised	Parallel to ground
Follow through	Yes	No	Yes	Yes	Yes
Part of ball hit	Center	Just below center	Halfway between center and top	Halfway between center and top	Center

ner through the wicket, he or she becomes alive again on all balls. The peeled ball gets credit for running the wicket but earns no bonus stroke.

You might also try a peel shot after you have roqueted a partner ball into position in front of a wicket. For the ensuing croquet shot, place your ball directly behind the partner ball, making sure they touch. To align this shot, picture parallel lines running along both sides of the ball. When you mentally extend those lines, they should pass through the wicket. Do this visualization from the back of the wicket, too.

Because this is a peel shot, it is a given that you want to hit this partner ball through the wicket. But what about the striker's ball? Perhaps it is shooting a different wicket than the object ball. If so, the peel may also be a split shot that moves the partner ball through the wicket and moves the striker's ball somewhere else.

If you do wish to run the wicket with your own ball, you have two choices. If you are not too close to the wicket, you may hit a stop shot, rolling the object ball through but holding your ball in the *approach zone.* From there, you can run the wicket on the continuation shot. If you are quite close to the wicket, you may roll-shot both balls through the wicket.

Practice. Place an object ball one to three feet directly in front of a wicket. Distance will vary with skill level, size of wicket, and quality of court, but you would be wise to start close enough to assure at least occasional success. Place your ball behind and touching the object ball. Now hit a dozen roll shots in which you try to roll both balls through the wicket. Then hit a dozen stop shots, striving to roll the object ball through the wicket while leaving the striker's ball near its starting point. Increase the distance only as you develop competence.

Next move the object ball so that it is no longer directly in front of the wicket. Start with just a slight angle. Hit a dozen split shots, trying to peel the object ball through the wicket and your ball to a chosen spot elsewhere. Again, increase the angle only as you achieve success.

Cannon

This is a shot involving three balls in which you hit (cannon) a croqueted ball into a third ball upon which your ball may be dead.

For example, suppose that the ball upon which you are about to take croquet is in front of but at a slight angle to the wicket, and that a third ball lies in the jaws of the wicket. Because your ball is dead on the ball in the jaws, you can't hit it directly without penalty; but you can cannon the croqueted ball into it.

Practice. Set up three balls as described in the previous example: target ball in the jaws, about-to-be-croqueted ball indirectly in front of the wicket. Place the striker's ball behind and touching the about-to-be-croqueted ball, so that an imaginary line extends through both balls to the ball in the jaws. Hit a series of shots, trying to cannon the target ball through the wicket, the croqueted ball off to the side (*stymied,* if possible, by the wicket wire), and your ball in front of the wicket, ready to run it on the continuation stroke. Increase distance and angle as you improve.

If you ask top croquet players what it takes to be an accomplished shot-maker, they will answer as one: "Practice." Without the ability to hit the shots, issues such as equipment, strategy, and mental tenacity have little importance.

STRATEGY

···

*It's-called croquet. It's something like golf
only it's fun.*

—*Dennis the Menace*,
by Hank Ketchum

"Strategy" refers to weighty decisions such as, Which ball should I hit? Which shot should I attempt? Where do I want to leave the balls at the end of my turn? How can I avoid getting my butt kicked?

At first, when you are trying to develop command over your shots, strategy is of little importance. You may use beginning tactics against an opponent, who will likely do the same against you.

Once the shots are mastered, ironically, croquet becomes more than just slam-bang offense. At its best, it is a fascinating mix of offense and defense, attack and defend. If the game were nothing more than smacking balls through wickets, it would hold no more interest than, say, bowling. But it is also a game of trying to prevent your opponent from smacking balls through wickets. Success demands striking a balance between offensive and defensive tactics.

Begin by realistically assessing your own shot-making ability and tactical skills. Then try to make the same analysis of your opponent. Keep in mind your respective levels of play when devising and revising strategy. For every shot, weigh the probable results of success versus the probable results of failure. Now, within those guidelines, attack! You will get better only by taking chances.

OPENINGS

In the American six-wicket game, all balls are dead until they run the first wicket. Thus, nothing should dissuade you from heading right for the first wicket. Jockeying for opening position is unnecessary, as there is no risk of being roqueted or leaving your opponent an easy break.

In the British (international) game, however, all balls are alive when the game begins. Experienced croquet players at that level typically open by hitting far away from the first wicket to one sideline or the other. Sometimes they will leave their ball tantalizingly close, trying to entice the opponent into a low-percentage shot.

If you are new to British rules, you may be tempted to shoot for the first wicket. If you are playing against another beginner, you may as well do just that. But if you aim for the first wicket against an experienced player, your chances of running the hoop are miniscule compared to your chances of leaving an easy break for your opponent.

In nine-wicket croquet, no such strategy should interfere. Attack right from the gate.

BREAKS

Playing good croquet requires the foresight of a chess player. The primary offensive strategy for players above beginner level is to use two or three other balls on the court to set up *breaks*—that is, to run multiple wickets in a single turn. By placing those balls at wickets ahead of the striker's next wicket, a player has a chance to run the court in one *all-round break*.

An alternative—favored by the Aunt Emma play-it-safe school of croquet—is to focus excessively on preventing the opponent from advancing. This strategy inhibits experimentation, retards the development of skills, and adds immeasurably to the tedium of the games played in this manner. Beginners who compete against players at their own level may achieve limited success with an Aunt Emma approach, but they will fare poorly against better players.

A player who wants to improve must play an attacking style. That means creating and playing breaks.

Two-ball breaks

The two-ball break, involving the striker's ball and one other, is the simplest to understand but the most difficult to execute. Because only two balls are used, each shot must be extremely accurate; the slightest error can end the break.

To practice a two-ball break, all you need are two wickets, two balls, and a spot of lawn. Place the balls as in figure 21, with yellow about six feet in front of a wicket and red a foot behind yellow. Playing red, you have a rush on yellow to the wicket. Gently rush yellow so that it stops about two feet in front of the wicket and six inches to one side.

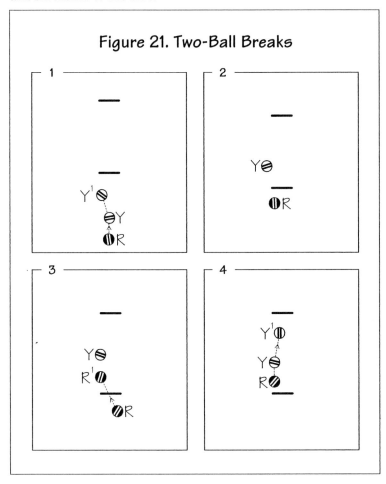

Figure 21. Two-Ball Breaks

Having roqueted yellow, you now take croquet on that ball. Place red in contact with yellow so that the V in between the balls points to one side of the wicket—in this case, to the left. With a stop shot, send red to a foot or two in front of the wicket and yellow well beyond it. With your continuation shot, run the hoop with red, hitting it hard enough to stop it just behind yellow. Then rush yellow to the second wicket. Repeat as necessary.

This two-ball break illustrates the first important principle of break play. You need a ball other than the striker's ball near the next hoop, so that the striker's ball can use it to play an approach shot to that wicket.

To sustain a two-ball break, every shot must be dead accurate or you will break down. You must rely on good rushes to the next wicket, which demands pinpoint control. Thus, it is usually preferable to construct a three- or four-ball break.

Three-ball breaks

A three-ball break is easier to sustain than a two-ball break, because it offers an extra stepping stone.

Returning to our previous example, red roquets yellow, then croquets yellow on to hoop three. Red then runs hoop one, earning a bonus stroke and leaving red in good position to roquet black. Red roquets black. Taking croquet on black, red is sent to a spot in front of hoop two and black is sent beyond hoop two on the side closest to hoop three. Red runs hoop two, making it alive on all balls, then roquets black again. On the ensuing croquet shot, red sends black to the fourth wicket, leaving itself a rush on yellow to the third hoop. Thus, black, the pioneer at hoop two, continues as the pioneer at hoop four. Red next roquets yellow. In taking croquet on yellow, red makes an approach shot that will enable it to run hoop three, sending yellow to hoop five.

Four-ball breaks

Figure 23 shows the initial ball placement. Yellow plays a split-shot approach, runs wicket one, then roquets red again. Yellow is put in contact with red for the croquet shot. A half roll is played, sending red as a pioneer to wicket three and yellow to black in the middle.

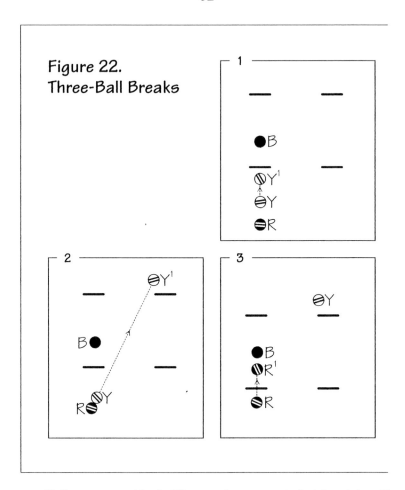

Figure 22.
Three-Ball Breaks

Yellow roquets black. The ensuing croquet shot is a take-off, sending yellow to blue and leaving black in the middle of the court. Yellow roquets blue, plays an approach shot to wicket two, runs it, and roquets blue again. Placing yellow behind blue, the striker hits another half roll, sending blue as a pioneer to hoop four and yellow to black.

After a roquet on black, yellow plays a take-off to red, roquets it, and the break continues. If yellow manages to make all twelve wickets, yellow is said to have made an *all-round four-ball break*. Drinks are on yellow.

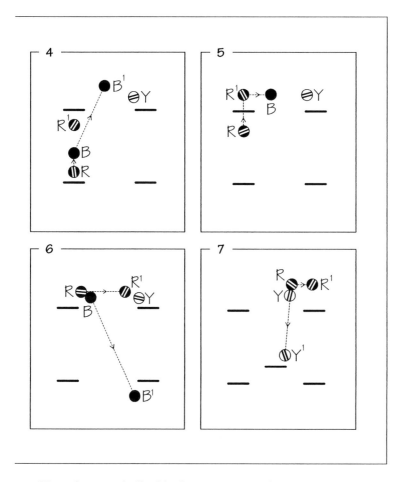

Note that one ball—black in our example—remains close to the center of the court. This is called the *pivot* ball, and ideally it should be on the same side of the stake as the wicket you just made. You can move it around the stake by playing take-offs from it or by roqueting it.

Though more complicated in concept, the four-ball break is the easiest break to accomplish. The most important shots to practice for a four-ball break are roquets, hoop shots, half rolls, thin take-offs, and approach shots. Work on your body English, too.

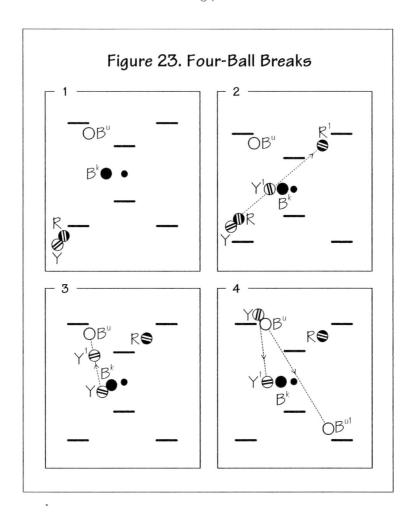

Figure 23. Four-Ball Breaks

DEFENSE

Although you should generally play an attacking game—especially as a beginner intent on mastering shots—you can't ignore
defense. The last strokes of a turn determine the position of the
balls faced by your opponent at the start of his or her turn. That
position is called the *leave*. The art of preparing the leave is
known as *laying up*.

Keep in mind the following four important principles of break play:

1. To run a wicket, you should have a ball other than the striker's ball near that wicket. You can move it there as needed or well in advance, in which case it is called a *pioneer*.
2. After running a wicket, send the pioneer ball to be a pioneer two wickets ahead. After running wicket four, for example, you would want to send the pioneer to wicket six (4 + 2).
3. Use rushes to make the croquet strokes in the break easier.
4. Play your strokes so that the subsequent strokes become shorter and easier. This is known as "easier said than done."

Leaves

The ideal leave will:

1. Not leave your opponent an easy shot.
2. Not leave your opponent a chance at a break.
3. Give you a chance to progress, even if your opponent plays the best defensive shot.

Tactically, you may want to do any or all of the following:

1. Put distance between the balls the opposing team is playing.
2. Leave your own balls (singles) close together, so that you have an easy roquet at the start of your next turn (provided you are alive on your own ball).
3. Take an opponent out of position to run the next wicket. If the opponent's ball is dead on two or three balls and can be kept that way, the opponent has lost much offensive potential.

4. Place your ball and your partner ball near a boundary line, far from opponent balls. This makes it hard for an opponent to pick up a break.

5. Place your ball so that it tempts your opponent to take a dangerous shot—that is, one that if missed will improve your chances of a break. That tempting shot is called a *tice*.

6. Try to leave your opponent's balls where they can most benefit you—for example, as pioneers near hoops you want to make.

7. Try to leave yourself a rush to somewhere useful.

8. Avoid leaving balls near your opponent's wicket.

9. *Wire* your opponent—place balls so that a wicket or stake obstructs your opponent's shot.

The first three points should always be followed. It will not always be possible to adhere to the others, but the closer you come, the better will be your defensive game.

END GAME

If you are playing two balls and make an all-round break with your first ball, don't stake out the rover and take it out of the game. It's a disadvantage to have one ball against an opponent's two. Instead, use your rover to help set up a break for your other ball; try to stake out both balls in the same turn.

WINNING THE MENTAL GAME

....

American croquet is more a game of
strategy and proper attitude than a game
of shot making.
　　　　　—Garth Eliassen, editor of the
　　　　　　　　　　National Croquet Calendar

You will inevitably master the physical skills of croquet long
before the mental skills. The standard line around the
greensward is that "croquet is ninety percent mental." But that's
only after you put in the practice time and master the strokes.
You can become a reasonably good stroke player in a couple of
years, but it usually takes at least five years of top-flight competition to be able to win a major event. First you learn to hit the
shots, then you learn to "think" in croquet.

It's often said that croquet is a blend of putting, billiards, and
chess. All three—especially billiards and chess—are fairly cere-
bral activities that reward abstract, forward thinking. This mental aspect is the biggest attraction for true croquet aficionados.

Mallet star Rhys Thomas studies professional golfers for tips
on how they mentally prepare for the next shot. "Like golfers, croquet players have a lot of time in between shots," he says. "We
both line up our shots and address our balls. I look at how golfers
keep their emotions in check, how they stay level. To me, the
shots themselves are insignificant compared to the mental prepa-
ration that goes on in between the shots. Croquet at the top level
is ninety percent brain."

Even at a middling level, mastering the so-called inner
game of croquet can give you a competitive advantage. If you mentally fortify yourself with the techniques in this chapter,
you can become a better player—without ever hitting a single ball.
Strive for the three Cs: confidence, concentration, and consistency.

OUTPLAYER TACTICS

When you miss a shot in croquet you become the *outplayer*. In a backyard game, you will probably wait on the court for your opponent to miss. But at the club level, outplayers are expected to wait on the sidelines.

If you watch a quality croquet match, you can't help but notice the stoicism of the outplayers. They are as unflappable as stuffed birds. Since it's not uncommon for players to run several wickets in one prolonged turn, outplayers must learn to cool their heels on the sidelines.

At the 1994 World Croquet Championship, there was some prolonged heel-cooling. Some outplayers sat, some stood, but all paid quiet attention. "Good outplayers keep their own council," says Rhys Thomas. Australian Neil Spooner says that even during his longest stretches as an outplayer, he is in the match. Wayne Rodoni, winner of the 1993 U.S. Open, says that outplayers should be constantly figuring out what to do if the opponent misses the next shot. And then the shot after that. As the opponent makes each one, you have to recalculate.

Rhys Thomas's "Three Kinds of Croquet Cruelty":

1. **The cruelty of opponent versus opponent.**
2. **The cruelty of nature—what the weather or court can do to you.**
3. **The cruelty you inflict upon yourself—the inner cruelty.**

Focus is a delicate skill to master. Pay too much attention to the trees and you may miss the forest. Rodoni knows that—now. He learned it for good near the end of his quarter-final match at the 1994 World Croquet Championship. Intent on pulling out a come-from-behind victory, he accidentally ran the same wicket twice with the same ball. Mistake, match, tournament. "A rookie mistake," he called it later. "I was so pleased with my previous shot, advancing my partner ball to the next wicket. I just forgot what I was doing."

Rodoni did not realize he had erred until his opponent, a vigilant outplayer, called him on it. If the outplayer had not seen the error, it would have stood and the match would have continued as though no misplay had occurred.

It is important to remain (or regain) calm. Bad outplay is easily recognizable by the absence of calm. To be effective, you must keep a lid on your emotions—at least the counterproductive ones. Rhys Thomas tries to keep it light. "It's important to maintain your humor as an outplayer," he says. "There's a reason why you became the outplayer—you missed a shot. By all means, analyze the missed shot. But don't dwell on it."

Charlie Smith, a scratch (zero-handicap) American player, thinks a good outplayer maintains equanimity by incorporating a little pessimism into his outlook. "If you're playing a good player, you should hope for the best and expect the worst," he says. "I really believe the key is to give up hope as soon as possible. If you're sitting there rooting and rooting, your hopes rise and fall with each shot. By the end of the match, you're an emotional wreck. Better to say, 'This guy's a good player. He's going to beat me, so I might as well enjoy watching him play.' Before you know it, he screws up, and you're in."

Some players rely on gamesmanship in their outplay. The story is told of an outplayer who, while his opponent was in the middle of a break, began ostentatiously packing away his mallet. The player on the court could not help seeing this. Sure enough, he soon missed, and the outplayer was back in the game.

ATTITUDE

Rhys Thomas asserts that croquet is "the perfect test for anyone who seeks to improve temperament. Because to succeed means to have good temperament."

The sport would seem to weed out most of the seething volcanic types. It's not unknown, however, for tempers to flare in croquet. Wayne Rodoni recalls a player who missed a comparatively easy shot in a tournament and "launched his mallet about fifty feet over the nearest fence. That's considered bad etiquette." Other players have heaved mallets at gophers who surfaced at the wrong time.

The word around the greensward is that Brit John Walters became an improved player after a journey to the Far East, where he received what might be called a "spiritual tune-up." Adopting a more Zen-like approach to the game, he won the World Croquet Federation Championship in 1991.

CONCENTRATION

If you talk to athletes at any level of any sport, you will hear of the importance of concentration. It's at the heart of success in any endeavor, but never more so than in croquet.

Almost everyone knows that concentration has to do with paying attention. Does that mean consciously willing yourself to focus? A voice in your head screaming over and over, "Pay attention!" until you do? Maybe so—at first. But eventually you will learn to relax and do it naturally. Once you've mastered the strokes and know when to use them, you will turn over game control to your now well-developed instincts.

Your conscious mind, however, will continue to interfere. Consider this equation:

$$performance = potential - interference$$

Performance is how well you actually do. In other words, results. Potential is a measurement of the best performance you are capable of at any given moment. Interference is the mental static produced by the conscious mind. For example, when pressure is minimal, the mind may become distracted: "Wonder where Debbie is right now. . . . How about those Knicks? . . . . Gad, don't I look stunning in white!"

As pressure mounts, so do self-doubts and anxiety, two other prime causes of mental static. Again, the conscious mind dives in, usually to provide a litany of advice: "Tight on the left hand . . . easy with the right . . . deep breaths . . . eye on the ball . . . head down . . . slow backswing . . . follow through . . . whoops!"

With all that advice raining down on you, is it any wonder that you're tighter than last year's pants? Steve Mulliner and John McCullough, in their book *The World of Croquet,* describe the consequences of doing the tighten-up: "The unwanted contraction of only a few extra muscle fibers in the arms is sufficient to turn the mallet face off line by one or two degrees, and so cause a fourteen-yard roquet to be missed by several inches."

Returning to our equation (performance equals potential minus interference), it is clear that a reduction in mental interference will improve performance, even with no change in potential (that is, practice). In other words, get your head straight and you can become a better player without picking up a mallet.

But the overactive conscious mind does not react well to orders to butt out. It's like commanding yourself to sleep. Better to use deceit: Distract it by focusing on something only tangentially related to the task at hand. By giving the conscious mind something to contemplate, the subconscious is left unhindered to deal with the shot at hand.

Here are some ways to distract that pesky conscious mind:

- Swing by the numbers. Count to three each time you swing. Recite "one" at the end of the backswing, "two" on contact, "three" at the end of the follow-through. Try to synchronize sound with event. It's harder than you think, and the conscious mind should be fully engaged in trying to accomplish it. You may find that counting—"one, two, three . . . one, two, three"—lends your swing a rhythm it lacked.

- Positive association. Suppose you face a long roquet to stay in a match. Like everyone, you have made a few and missed a few. Focus on the good ones and forget the bad ones. Replay an imaginary tape entitled "My Greatest Hits." Immerse yourself in positive associations.

- Visualization. First cousin to positive association, visualization is a type of mental rehearsal in which you conjure up detailed visions of the activity before you do it.

    The first step is to relax. Use a method that works for you. You might close your eyes and take a few deep breaths. Play a mental videotape of a winning moment—from stalk to swing. You may see it from your own perspective or from someone else's, whichever seems more comfortable. Focus on the finer points of the swing. See it as one fluid whole. Hear the sounds, feel the heft of the mallet, your fingers curling around the shaft, the give of the grass. Immerse yourself in the swing; see the ball streaking toward its target, like a heat-seeking missile.

Visualization takes dedicated practice, but you can practice it anywhere—in the bathtub, at a bus stop— and the rewards can be staggering. I have interviewed and profiled forty world-class athletes, many of whom attribute some, if not most, of their success to visualization.

Research suggests that muscles respond to visualization of an act almost as if you actually had done the act. Thus, the more intensely you visualize the perfect stop shot, the more entrenched it will be in your muscle memory. This kind of memory operates almost entirely on the subconscious level, which helps explain how you can play a shot beautifully but can't explain it to others.

SUPERSTITION

Some croquet players build their confidence and mental toughness on the shaky foundation of superstition. It's not uncommon for a player to carry a lucky charm or a lucky quarter for the pregame coin toss. Some insist on wearing the same lucky clothes during a winning streak. One top-ranked American player believes that if he doesn't make his bed—even his hotel bed— some cruel indignity is bound to befall him on the croquet court. At least one player employs a hex. "If he really needs an advantage," says one of his opponents, "he does a flick of the thumb and forefinger, which, roughly translated, means, 'A pox on you!' More often than not, he gets what he wants."

One East Coast player reportedly declines to interrupt a winning streak with the mundane chore of washing his clothes. "If he's in the medals," says Rhys Thomas, "he's not the guy you want to be standing next to at the awards ceremony."

Thomas believes that experience eventually obviates superstitions. As players learn that their "lucky shirt" isn't foolproof, it ceases to be essential and is dropped. Before that, however, superstition can actually improve play, acting as kind of a placebo.

PRESSURE

As you improve and play better competition, the pressure mounts. It is pressure that causes a scratch player to stick a ball in the jaws from six inches away, a shot he has made a hundred times in a row. In fact, pressure can cause an accomplished player to go brain dead in the middle of a match. "I've seen great players go so brain dead they hit their opponent's ball," says Thomas.

To make sure that doesn't happen to you, use a mental checklist. Make it a habit, before every hit, to ask yourself the following questions:

- Is it really my turn?
- Am I hitting the right ball?
- Which wicket am I shooting?
- Who shoots after me?
- Can I do anything for my partner or partner ball?
- What do I really want to accomplish with this stroke?

It's important to go through the conscious (albeit silent or *sotto voce*) process of asking these questions. Once you've gained some experience, you will do it quickly. But even then, don't skip any steps.

Picture this scenario: You're behind in a match against a pretty good player in your neighborhood or club. You have a tough shot to stay in the game. There are a few people watching and the rivalry intensifies. Your gut's twisting like wet rope— that's pressure. Almost everyone feels it at one time or another. The real question is, Can you control it? Successful people don't dodge pressure; they make it work to their benefit.

On the other hand, it seems that some people just don't feel it at all. George Brett, destined for the Baseball Hall of Fame, was once asked about the pressure of playing his game. His response, as I paraphrase it, is equally applicable to croquet. "Pressure?" Brett said, "Ha, this isn't pressure. This is just a game. Pressure is feeding a family of four on a fixed income."

Words to remember.

GETTING BETTER

···

Do I drink the wine and then take my best
shot, or do I take my shot and then drink?
—Timothy White,
"Steve Winwood's Merging Traffic,"
Musician Magazine, July 1986

L et's say you're a capable backyard croquet player, the toast of
the neighborhood. You consistently beat all comers for three
blocks in any direction. Now you are toying with the notion of
joining a club and playing association croquet. Good plan. But
there are four changes you should make in your backyard game
to ease the transition.

1. Start playing six-wicket, one-stake croquet, using the
    configuration shown earlier. With few exceptions, that's
    the layout used everywhere croquet is played—except
    in American backyards. If you want to compete against
    capable players, you have to learn the six-wicket game.
2. Master the proper croquet stroke. If your ball hits
    another ball, you earn two shots, the first of which
    should be a true croquet shot, a two-ball stroke. Place
    your ball so that it is touching the ball you just hit (the
    roqueted ball), and, without the help of a controlling
    foot, strike your ball, moving both it and the other ball a
    predetermined direction and distance. Abandon the
    idea that croquet nirvana is placing your foot on your
    own ball and whacking your opponent into the cherry
    orchard.

    Your goal with the croquet shot is to position your
    ball for the best possible continuation shot and the
    roqueted ball for future use.

    The ability to control the movement of the two balls

when you take croquet is at the heart of excellence. Whether you're a backyard player or a club pro, your aim is to run multiple wickets in one turn. You can accomplish that only by moving partner and opponent balls to serve as stepping stones for running future wickets.

3. In singles, play two balls whenever possible. By providing more balls to be used as stepping stones, this method complicates strategy and increases possibilities.

4. Replace your wide wire wickets with narrower association wickets, or bend the wire ones so that they are only slightly wider than the balls. Shooting at smaller targets will improve your accuracy and assure that a lucky shot won't determine the outcome of the game. If you move up to association croquet, familiarity with the narrow wickets will be to your advantage.

Actually, while you're at it, move up to tournament balls and mallets. And how about reseeding the back lawn?

Perhaps the stories of three players who pursued excellence can be a guiding light.

Neil Spooner, who was born in Adelaide, South Australia, did not discover croquet until he was a student at Westminister College in Adelaide. "One day I was sitting in a classroom that overlooked a court where croquet was being played," he remembers. "I thought it looked interesting, so I switched to croquet for my activities period. That was the start.

"I joined a club that had floodlighting. In 1970, I went out every night for six months—paying sixty cents for lights—and practiced through rain and even hail. When I first started practicing, I played games against myself. I found I would try things I wouldn't try in a match. And by trying them, I found I could do them.

"I played with a handicap of fifteen in my first tournament. Within nine months, it was down to three. It took me another eight months to become a minus player. I modeled myself after John Magor, the best player in Australia. My goal was to be that good. Then to beat him, which I eventually did in 1977."

According to Spooner, the most common beginner trap is thinking the game is easy. "Beginners try difficult shots straight away," he says, "and when they fail, they get disappointed and quit. They don't realize how difficult it is. It's one of the most frustrating games in the world, croquet. To move to the next level—as with anything—you must practice. Play matches. Get experience. Enter tournaments."

One of only twenty-two scratch players in the United States, Charlie Smith was a young adult before he discovered croquet.

"I was playing golf one day with my father and brother," he says. "I was a terrible golfer, but my father loved the game, so I played to be around him. As we walked off the course, we saw someone fooling around on the croquet court and decided to check it out. It turned out to be Damon Bidencoat, a world-class player. He showed us how to do some things, and I thought it was kind of interesting. Then I saw Damon run six hoops in a row, and I thought, Wouldn't it be something to get to be that good?"

Motivation in place, Smith joined a club and began to practice. And practice. "If you enjoy the game," he says, "you don't need a partner to practice. It's like shooting hoops in basketball. You can go out and perfect the skills alone."

In his first tournament, he competed against a fifty-five-year-old woman who reduced him to what he calls "emotional rubble." He says, "I was unprepared for the kind of tension that can build in a croquet match. My knees and arms were shaking. My opponent was looking as grim as death out there, intimidating the hell out of me. But I won the match, and when I heard the applause from the crowd, I was totally hooked."

Smith believes the most common beginner mistake is letting yourself get too embarrassed by mistakes. "It's important for beginners to remember that no matter how egregious their error, there are far more experienced players making those exact same mistakes. They're just not making them as often. If you're interested in getting better, it's important to take risks. You'll take your lumps, but you'll learn. If you like competition, croquet is great. The competition is ferocious. I know that sounds strange, like saying bingo is a hairy game. But it's true."

Despite the intense competition in top-flight croquet, there is, says Smith, "a good spirit in this game. Veterans will frequently get on the court with rookies and help them out. It can be extraordinarily intimidating to play a top player. The thing is to try and learn from it. Don't get driven out of the game by that experience. Remember, the veteran wants the rookie to get better."

Wayne Rodoni, arguably America's best player, was also a young adult when he discovered croquet. His friend, Bruce, sold sporting equipment, and the two of them decided to order a croquet set. They began playing on Bruce's parents' back lawn. "It was a big lawn but not manicured," Rodoni recalls. "We began playing our own version of six-wicket croquet on warm summer evenings. We eventually found a rulebook and started playing the right way—with deadness and all. I got pretty good at hitting around the walnuts that littered the court. I was soon intrigued enough to take an introductory clinic at the San Francisco Croquet Club. That was six years ago and I'm still playing."

The most common beginner mistake, says Rodoni, is skipping the steps necessary to be good. "Some people never get a swing or a comfortable grip," he says. "They walk up, swing away, and wonder why they're not hitting well. They don't want to dedicate the time necessary. The game is not as easy as it looks. Still, there are a lot more good players now than six years ago. That's fortunate for new players. I learned a lot by getting beat by experienced top-quality players. You get pounded when you make a mistake against a good player."

Rodoni urges beginners to play a lot of golf croquet. "It develops single-ball shooting and hoop running," he says. "It teaches you how to swing the mallet properly. I know an instructor who starts beginners off with the geometry of split shots. They're not ready for that. First, you need to create a swing line, a sight line."

Actually, first you need to love the game.

RULES

···

One of the great things about croquet is its adaptability. You can play on any size court, with any size wickets, using golf clubs, flamingos, or real mallets, and still have a blast. You can allow foot shots or not, staple nylon string for boundaries or use a well-placed juniper bush, and as long as it's the same for both sides, you have a fair game.

But will it be the best game? Doubtful.

Croquet has evolved incrementally since the *Routledge Handbook of Croquet* first codified the rules in 1861. When the United States Croquet Association was formed in 1976, codifying the rules of the American six-wicket game was a top priority. Over the years, input from countless players—trial and error, in other words—has produced modifications that have improved the game. The USCA six-wicket game now differs significantly (carry-over deadness, for example) from the six-wicket game played in most other countries. The (British) Croquet Association rulebook may be purchased from the USCA for those interested in the International Rules (Association Laws) game.

As for the nine-wicket game, the changes go on. The USCA Nine-Wicket Rules Committee canvassed groups and clubs all around the country that play nine-wicket croquet, and the best of their rules have been assimilated into a revised 1995 rule book. They are presented here for the first time in a mainstream publication. It is the ardent hope of the USCA that such revisions will make the nine-wicket rules easier to understand, more fun to play, and ultimately more popular.

RULES OF AMERICAN NINE-WICKET CROQUET

Part 1: Overview

1. The game can be played by two to six players.
2. The game is designed to be played with six balls or four balls. It can be played between two sides or between

individuals (cutthroat), in which each player plays for him- or herself with no partner.

3. Wickets may be up to twice the diameter of the balls.

4. The game can be played on all terrains, but close-cropped grass is best.

5. Wicket clips are useful but optional.

6. The standard double diamond rectangular court may be adjusted to fit the size and shape of the space available. In ideal situations, refer to the nine-wicket court diagram on page 8, which shows a 50 foot x 100 foot court with boundaries. Marked boundaries are optional.

7. A game usually requires from one to two hours to play to conclusion—that is, until one of the two sides has "staked out" by striking the finishing stake with each ball on the team.

8. In games with time limits, the winner is determined by counting points (see rule 10 below) to see which side has progressed the farthest around the court at the moment time has expired.

9. Each stake hit or wicket made in the proper order counts as one point.

10. Each ball in a game can score sixteen points for its side, fourteen wicket points and two stake points. In the six-ball game, there are forty-eight points that can be scored by each side (three balls to a team). In the four-ball game, there are thirty-two points that can be scored by each side (two balls to a team).

Part 2: The Teams

11. When playing with six balls, the order of play is blue, red, black, yellow, green, and orange. When playing with four balls, the order is blue, red, black, and yellow.

12. In team play with six balls, one team plays blue, black, and green while the other plays red, yellow, and orange.

13. In team play with four balls, one side plays blue and black while the other plays red and yellow.

14. In singles, one person plays all the balls of one side. It is

recommended that the four-ball version be used in singles, blue and black opposite red and yellow.

15. In doubles, there are two players per side, each playing one ball. It is recommended that the four-ball version be used in doubles, as in singles.

16. In triples, there are three players per side, each playing one ball. It is recommended that the six-ball version be used.

17. In individual (cutthroat) play, each player is playing for him- or herself with no partner. It is recommended that the six-ball version be used.

.18. In games for two, four, or six people, players play in regular sequence, playing the correct ball in rotation. If there are three or five players, two players should be on one side and one or three on the other. The players on the side with two people play in order, hitting their balls in correct rotation. The other side can play in the following manner: On a side with one player, that player plays two balls; on a side with three players, one player plays one ball and the other two players share a ball.

Part 3: Commencing Play

19. A coin toss is used to determine which side goes first.

20. Each of the balls is brought into play in the first six turns, beginning thirty-six inches directly in front of the "starting stake."

Part 4: The Turn

21. In a six-ball game, the order of play is blue, red, black, yellow, green, and orange.

22. In a four-ball game, the order of play is blue, red, black, and yellow.

23. At the conclusion of a turn in which a wicket or stake point is scored, the wicket clip of the color correspond-

ing to the ball should be placed on the next wicket or stake to be scored by that ball.

24. If your set does not include wicket clips, you may use colored clothespins.

Part 5: Bonus Strokes

25. There are two ways to earn bonus strokes:
     a) Scoring a wicket or hitting the turning stake gives you one bonus stroke.
     b) Roqueting (hitting) a ball with the striker's ball gives you two bonus strokes.

26. All wicket or stake bonus strokes must be played from where the ball lies after the point is made.

27. After roqueting a ball, a player has four options:
     a) Take the two bonus strokes starting from where the player's ball has come to rest.
     b) With ball-in-hand, place the player's ball one mallet head's length away from the other (roqueted) ball in any direction and then take two bonus strokes.
     c) With ball-in-hand, place the player's ball in contact with the struck ball (where it has come to rest), then strike the player's ball so as to send both balls in the desired direction. This is called "taking croquet."
     d) With ball-in-hand, place the player's ball in contact with the struck ball (where it has come to rest), and resting the player's foot on his own ball so as to render it immobile, strike the player's own ball so as to send the other ball off in the desired direction. The player's own ball remains where it is, and the player has one more bonus stroke remaining. If the player's ball moves from under the foot, there is no penalty and the bonus stroke is taken.

28. Each ball may be roqueted for bonus strokes only once in a turn, unless the striker scores a wicket or strikes the turning stake, in which case the balls may be roqueted again for bonus strokes.

29. Bonus strokes may not be accumulated. Only the last

earned bonus strokes may be played. There are two exceptions to this rule:

a) If you score both wickets at the starting and turning stakes.

b) If, with a single stroke, you run a wicket and hit another ball.

T he USCA and most croquet teachers advise seri-
ous players to opt for the contact rule—that is, to take croquet. Only then will you improve your two-ball shots and better prepare yourself for the Association level of play.

Contact rule.

a) To take croquet, the striker's ball shall be placed on the ground in contact at any point with the roqueted ball, but not in contact with any other ball.

b) Before a croquet shot, the striker may touch or steady the roqueted ball and may further apply such pressure by hand or foot, but not by mallet, as is reasonably necessary to make it hold its position.

c) Before a croquet shot, the striker shall not intentionally move any ball but his own, but if another ball is moved unintentionally, the striker shall replace the ball without penalty.

d) In a croquet shot, the croqueted ball must visibly move. Failure to move the croqueted ball is a fault.

e) After the croquet shot, the striker may take a continuation shot unless another roquet is made, in which case two shots are again earned and croquet is taken from the roqueted ball.

f) The striker may not place a hand or foot on a ball during the croquet shot.

30. Roqueting a ball a second time in a turn without having yet scored a wicket or stake point is not a fault, but you do not receive additional bonus strokes as a result of the second roquet. Play proceeds from where the balls came to rest.

31. If another player (partner or opponent) puts your ball through its proper wicket or into the turning stake, your side gets the point but no bonus stroke.

32. If a player roquets more than one ball in a stroke, it gets bonus strokes from the first ball roqueted, with the other balls remaining where they came to rest.

33. Playing the game with "deadness" is optional. See part 9 for an explanation.

Part 6: Rover Balls

34. Rovers are balls that have completed the entire course except for striking the finishing stake.

35. Rovers may be staked out—that is, driven into the finishing stake with any legal stroke by any player at any point in the game.

36. Rovers can roquet the other balls only once in a turn to receive bonus strokes.

37. The purpose of the rover is to help your partner and hinder your opponents.

38. A rover can score a point only by staking out at the finishing stake. It is then removed from the game.

Part 7: Boundaries and Out-of-Bounds

39. String or painted boundaries are not essential. Natural boundaries, such as bushes and trees, can be used.

40. It is recommended that boundaries be at least six feet away from the outer wickets.

41. A ball sent out of bounds can be brought in with no penalty. Place the ball thirty-six inches inside the

boundary line from the point of exit. If the player has a second bonus shot, he or she then plays it.

Note: Although six-wicket croquet mallets are three feet long and therefore suitable for measuring where to place an out-of-bounds ball, backyard mallets can be up to a foot shorter. One solution is to cut a couple of three-foot measuring sticks and keep them handy.

42. All balls that come to rest within the boundary margin (closer than one mallet length to the boundary) are repositioned at a spot three feet from the boundary.

Part 8: Faults and Penalties

43. You must strike the ball squarely with the face of the mallet only.
44. The mallet may not hit another ball when striking the ball you are playing.
45. The mallet may not hit the wicket or stake to cause another ball to move.
46. If a fault occurs, as in the above, all balls are replaced and the turn ends.
47. Unless there is a referee, the word of the players should be taken in disputes.
48. If a ball is played out of turn, it is not a fault. The ball or balls are replaced and the proper ball then plays.

Part 9: Deadness (optional)

49. A ball is "dead" on another ball when it roquets the ball during a turn. You do not become "alive" and able to roquet that ball again until you have been through a wicket in proper sequence or until you have hit the turning stake. A rover ball may become alive by going through any wicket in any direction but may still only roquet the other balls once per turn. The deadness option allows for more complex strategy.

The American notion of "deadness" is different from the British (or international) version. In the American game, if you acquire deadness on a ball, you remain dead on it until you have cleared the next wicket or hit the turning stake. In international play, you are alive on every ball with each new turn, regardless of whether or not you have cleared a wicket.

Some believe that this rule difference tends to make American players more conservative. They are afraid to hit balls, for to do so makes them dead on those balls. Their English counterparts, alive with each new turn, attempt more ambitious roquets—and become better at them.

GOLF CROQUET

Golf croquet is a fun, effective modification of regulation croquet. It introduces new players to a croquet court and teaches them the sequence of wickets. It allows them to practice basic croquet strokes, such as rushes, and teaches them the importance of hitting balls to specific spots.

The basic rules are as follows:

1. Singles or doubles may be played. As in regular croquet, red and yellow play blue and black.
2. Balls begin one mallet length from the center stake (six-wicket croquet) or from either stake (nine-wicket).
3. There are no bonus strokes—and therefore no roquet, croquet, or continuation shots. Each ball is hit only once per turn, in sequence, as seen in descending order on the stake: blue, red, black, and yellow. A player may choose to waive (pass) the turn and not strike the ball.

4. The winner of a wicket is the side that runs the wicket in the fewest number of strokes. Like golf, everyone is going for the hole at the same time. Unlike golf, balls are allowed to interfere with each other.

5. The first ball to run the first wicket in the correct direction scores one point for its side. The contest for that wicket is finished.

6. From where they lie, the balls are next played toward wicket two. The order of play is continued; so, for example, if black runs hoop one, yellow hits first toward hoop two.

7. If a striker's ball partly runs a wicket, it may run the wicket on a subsequent turn and score the point, unless the point has already been scored. The wicket point can be scored by a ball that is cannoned, peeled, or knocked through a wicket by an opponent or partner.

8. A player may get a head start on the next wicket to be played, but the wicket cannot be scored if the previous wicket has not yet been scored.

9. If a player hits out of turn or hits the wrong ball, there is no penalty, except that stroke and any strokes thereafter are canceled. Balls are returned to their position before the error, and play is resumed by the correct player playing the correct ball. No points scored during the period of error shall be counted.

10. A player cannot deliberately make his ball leave the ground. That is, there are no jump shots. (This inflates the value of stymies.) Even if the striker does so accidentally, cancel any goals scored on the illegal hit. If an illegal jump shot displaces other balls, the displaced team can either accept the new position or replace.

11. If a ball runs two wickets in one stroke, score two points for that side.

12. The game ends as soon as one side has scored a majority of the points to be played (e.g., a seven-point game is over when one side scores four points).

 a) In a short version, seven points are contested—the first six wickets and the stake.

    b) In a medium version, thirteen points are contested—twelve wickets and the stake.

    c) In a long version, nineteen points are contested—eighteen wickets and the stake.

        Realistically, any odd number of wickets and stakes will work. Or you can play a time limit.

13. Consider giving handicaps (bisques) depending on the length of the game and the relative skill levels.

Advanced Play

In advanced play, the above rules apply, with the following exceptions:

1) Rule 7 is modified so that if a striker causes one of the balls of his or her side partly to run a wicket, such a ball must start over in order to run that wicket on a subsequent shot. If, on the other hand, an opponent causes a ball partly to run a wicket, that ball may run the wicket on its next shot.

2) Rule 8 is modified so that you must contest the wickets in order even if one seems to be a lost cause. That is, you cannot strategically send a ball to the next hoop. If you do so deliberately, your ball is replaced and you lose your turn.

GLOSSARY

alive: In American play, a ball that has cleared a wicket but has not yet roqueted a ball is said to be alive on that ball. In the British game, all balls are alive at the start of every turn.

all-round break: Running all the wickets in a single turn.

angle of divergence: Angle at which balls separate when a croquet shot is made.

approach shot: A shot designed to move a ball into position to clear the next wicket or to roquet another ball.

Association croquet: British-rules game played in all croquet countries except the United States. Many Americans play both Association and USCA croquet.

Aunt Emma: A dull, conservative, uninspired player.

ball-in-hand: A ball that has made a roquet, or gone out of bounds, which the striker is entitled to pick up and move.

bisque *(take over)***:** Difference between two players' handicaps; the number of extra turns given a weaker player to equalize play.

block *(stymie)***:** Obstruction of the striker's ball by a ball upon which it is dead.

bonus stroke: An extra stroke earned by running a hoop or making a roquet (two bonus strokes).

break: A series of wickets scored by a player in one turn using one other ball **(two-ball break)**, two other balls **(three-ball break)**, or three other balls **(four-ball break)**.

break down: To commit a fault or make an unsuccessful shot, causing a turn to end.

cannon shot: A combination shot in which the striker's ball drives one ball into another ball.

carom shot: A shot in which the striker's ball glances off a wicket, stake, or other ball before hitting a ball.

carrying through: Leading with the arms on the follow-through.

center stance: The traditional striker's stance in which the mallet is swung between the legs.

clearing *(cleaning)***:** Becoming alive on all other balls by running a wicket.

clips: Plastic or metal markers colored to match the balls. In club or tournament play, they are clipped to the next wicket to be run by that color ball. Markers are clipped to the top of the hoop on the first half of the course and to an upright on the return circuit.

condone: To let an opponent's foul go unclaimed. An unclaimed foul becomes a legal play, with no penalty on the striker.

continuation shot: An extra shot earned by clearing a wicket; the shot taken after the croquet shot.

Croquet Association (CA): British croquet governing body, founded as the All-England Croquet Club.

croqueted ball: In a croquet shot, the ball that is moved but not struck by the striker.

croquet stroke: The stroke earned by making a roquet. The striker's ball is placed in contact with the roqueted ball, and a hit is made that moves, or at least shakes, both balls.

cross-wire: To position the opponent's balls on opposite sides of a wicket or stake, thus preventing one from hitting the other.

crown: The top part of a wicket.

crush stroke: A fault in which the striker's mallet is in contact with the striker's ball at the same time the ball is in contact with a wicket or stake. It can happen when a striker forces the mallet after the ball while trying to run a wicket from a few inches away.

cut rush: A roquet in which the striker's ball hits the roqueted ball (rushed ball) off center, causing it to travel at a desired angle.

deadness: The state of a ball that has hit (roqueted) another ball. It is said to be *dead* on that ball, and that deadness cannot be cleared until after the next wicket is cleared (American) or a new turn is started (British).

deadness board: A display with colored markers to help players and spectators keep track of deadness.

double tap: A fault in which the striker accidentally hits the ball twice in the same stroke.

double target: Two balls sitting so close together that the target area is more than doubled.

drive shot: A croquet shot in which both balls travel in the same direction, with the croqueted ball moving about three times farther than the striker's ball.

fault: An unacceptable stroke, which, if caught, results in a foul and penalty.

foot shot: A shot taken with the striker's foot resting on his or her ball to hold it in place. Legal only in backyard croquet.

forestall: To prevent a player from committing a fault.

four-ball break: Running multiple wickets on one turn using four balls.

garden croquet: Another name for nine-wicket backyard croquet.

golf style: A method of hitting in which the mallet passes in front of the body like a golf club.

grip: The manner in which a croquet mallet is held.

groom the court *(create a leave)*: To place balls so as to leave the partner ball a good playing opportunity and the opponent a bad one.

hampered *(hoop bound)*: The condition of a striker when a wicket or stake interferes with a normal swing.

heel: The mallet face that does not strike the ball in a particular stroke.

hitting true: Striking the ball with a level swing, in contrast to hitting up or down.

hoop: English term for *wicket*.

Irish grip: A grip in which both palms face outward, as in the classic golf grip.

jaws: Entrance to the uprights of a wicket.

join up: To position your ball near your partner ball.

jump shot: A shot made with a downward stroke that causes the striker's ball to leave the ground and, if done correctly, to avoid an obstructing ball, stake, or wicket.

lay a break: To position balls at future wickets to set up a possible break.

lay up: To prepare a leave.

leave: The position of balls after a turn.

level play: Competition with no handicaps.

limit of claims: The time frame during which a fault may be called.

MacRobertson Shield: An international croquet competition held every few years between Great Britain, Australia, New Zealand, and, most recently, the United States.

nine-wicket croquet: A variation of croquet in which nine wickets and two stakes are positioned in a "double-diamond" configuration. This variation is popular in American backyards.

out of bounds: Status of a ball whose vertical axis has crossed a boundary line.

pass: To waive or pass up a turn.

pass roll: A shot that sends the striker's ball farther than the croqueted ball.

peel: To cause a ball other than one's own to run the proper wicket.

penultimate: The next-to-last wicket.

pioneer ball: In a three- or four-ball break, the ball sent ahead to the wicket after the one the player is attempting to run.

pivot ball: The middle ball in a four-ball break. Positioned near the center stake, preferably on the side being played, it is roqueted before roqueting the pioneer ball.

playing side: Area in front of the approach side of a wicket.

push: To keep the mallet head on the ball after initial contact. It is allowed only on the croquet shot, and only if the mallet head does not speed up after making contact.

roll shot: A croquet shot in which both balls travel along the same line (e.g., *half roll, full roll, pass roll*).

roquet: A shot in which the striker's ball contacts another ball upon which it is alive. Except in some backyard games, it is followed by a croquet shot and a continuation shot.

Routledge's Handbook of Croquet: An English publication written by Edmund Routledge in 1861 that is believed to be the sport's first rulebook. It still governs croquet today, albeit with numerous modifications.

rover: A ball that has cleared all wickets but has not yet hit the finishing stake. Like a king in checkers, the rover is free to go anywhere.

rover hoop: The last wicket before the final stake.

run a wicket: To hit a ball through a wicket in the proper order and direction. When the ball comes to rest, it must have cleared the plane of the playing side of the wicket.

rush: A roquet shot in which the striker attempts to send the roqueted ball to a predetermined position.

rush line: An imaginary line extending from the ball about to be rushed to its intended destination.

scratch player: A player with a zero handicap.

sequence game: A croquet match in which the turns are played in sequence determined by ball color (usually blue, red, black, yellow). The American game, unlike the British game, is a strict sequence game.

side stance: A stance in which the mallet is swung alongside the body (contrast with *center stance*).

sight line: A line inscribed lengthwise on top of the mallet head to help the striker aim.

single-ball stroke: A stroke that causes only one ball to move.

Solomon grip: A grip in which both palms face inward.

split shot: A croquet stroke that sends the striker's ball and the croqueted ball in different directions.

stake *(peg)*: A round wooden stick painted with colored stripes. In the nine-wicket game, there are two stakes, a starting/finishing stake and an upper or turning stake. In the six-wicket game, there is one center finishing stake.

stake out *(peg out)*: The final shot for any ball.

stalk: To line up a shot by approaching your ball from behind it.

stance: The position of the striker's feet and body in relation to the line of the mallet swing.

standard grip *(reverse-palm grip)*: A grip in which one palm faces inward and the other faces outward.

sticky wicket: Having a tough approach to a wicket; being stuck in a wicket.

stop shot: A croquet shot that sends the croqueted ball much farther than the striker's ball.

striker: The player whose turn it is.

stroke: Mallet movement that deliberately or accidentally moves a ball. Also a swing that misses all balls.

stymie *(block)*: A ball blocking the intended path of the striker's ball when the striker's ball is dead on it.

take-off shot: A croquet shot in which the croqueted ball moves very little and the striker's ball moves a greater distance.

take over: A *bisque*.

three-ball break: Running multiple wickets on one turn using three balls.

tice: A shot that positions the striker's ball where it will entice an opponent to shoot at it and miss.

time limit: An alternative way of ending a game or match. In tournament play, the time limit is usually about an hour and a half. There may also be a time limit for individual shots—often forty-five seconds.

toe: The mallet face used to strike the ball in a particular shot.

two-ball stroke: A croquet stroke.

two-ball break: Running multiple wickets on one turn using two balls.

United States Croquet Association (USCA): The American croquet governing body, founded in New York in 1976.

waive: To pass up a turn.

wicket: A straight- or curved-top arch through which balls are driven (*hoop* in England).

wired ball: A ball obstructed by a wicket, stake, or ball upon which it is dead that cannot be hit by the striker's ball.

RESOURCES

··

CLUBS

Suppose you want to become more seriously involved in croquet. What do you do? Step one: Start hanging out with people who share your enthusiasm for the sport. In other words, join a club. To do so:

1. Start your own club. About 20 percent of the more than three hundred USCA member-clubs are home based. They typically have a one- or two-family core, with neighbors or other family members joining as their interest grows.
2. Join a private croquet club. This is typically an organized group of ten to one hundred members, usually adults who enjoy both the competitive and the social benefits of the game. They usually play on more formal, well-kept courts.
3. Join a country club, tennis club, or sports club that, although dominated by other sports, offers croquet to its members.
4. Attend a school or college that has a club or team. Many East Coast schools field croquet teams.
5. Join a retirement community that has croquet courts.

Peruse the following list of clubs registered with the United States Croquet Association to determine whether there are any in your neighborhood. In some cases, the club's physical location differs from its mailing address. In those instances, the club's physical location is given in parentheses right after its name. Not listed are college teams and clubs so exclusive that they decline to publish any information.

To learn more about clubs, to update information, or to receive organizational assistance, contact the United States Croquet Association (USCA) at 500 Avenue of the Champions, Palm Beach Gardens, FL 33418, telephone 407-627-3999. The executive director is Dean Reinke, but other members of the friendly, informative staff can help you.

The USCA can also provide instructional materials, educational clinics, tournament formats, discounts on croquet equipment, and subscriptions to the *U.S. Croquet Gazette*. These benefits easily justify the annual dues.

THE USCA MEMBER-CLUB DIRECTORY

ALASKA
- Choccolocco Croquet Club, Anniston.
- Pond House Croquet Club, Pell City.

ARIZONA
- Arizona Croquet Club, Phoenix.
- Downtown Croquet Club, Phoenix.
- Gainey Estate Club, Scottsdale.

CALIFORNIA
- Beverly Hills Croquet Club (Roxbury Park), Santa Monica.
- Calabasas Croquet Club, Calabasas.
- Casa Woodfin Croquet Club, Indian Wells.
- Croquet Club of Carmel, Carmel.
- Fairbanks Ranch Country Club, Rancho Santa Fe.
- Fox Hollow Croquet Club, Sacramento.
- Indian Ridge Country Club, Palm Desert.
- Ink Grade Group, Pope Valley.
- Joslyn Cove, Indian Wells.
- Long Beach Croquet Club, Long Beach.
- Marin Croquet Club, Mill Valley.
- Marlborough Court, Oakland.
- Marrakesh Country Club, Palm Desert.
- Meadowood Croquet Club, St. Helena.
- Mission Hills Croquet Club, Rancho Mirage.
- Nellie Gail Croquet Club, Laguna Hills.
- Newton Croquet Club, St. Helena.
- Oak Creek Croquet Club, Palo Alto.
- Oakland Croquet Club, Concord.
- Park Chevron Croquet Club, San Ramon.
- Park Newport Croquet Club, Newport Beach.
- Rancho Santa Fe Croquet Club, Rancho Santa Fe.
- Rancho Valencia Croquet Club, Rancho Santa Fe.
- San Francisco Croquet Club, San Francisco.
- Smoke Tree Ranch, Palm Springs.
- Star Farms Hay and Croquet Club, San Miguel.
- Western Croquet Club (Windsor/Sonoma-Cutrer Winery), Rohnert Park.
- Yolo Polo Croquet and Bocce Club, Woodland.

COLORADO
- Denver Croquet Club, Denver.

CONNECTICUT
- Compo Beach Mallet Club, Westport.
- Easton Lawn Club, Easton.
- Gray Gables Croquet Club, Old Lyme.
- Greenwich Croquet Club (Greenwich), Darien.
- Money Point Mallet Club, Mystic.

DISTRICT OF COLUMBIA
- Capital City Croquet Club (Washington, D.C.), Falls Church.

DELAWARE

- Delaware Croquet Club, Wilmington.
- Vicmead Mallet Club (Wilmington), Rockland.

FLORIDA

- Associated Marine Institutes, Tampa.
- Audubon Croquet Club, Naples.
- Beach Club, Palm Beach.
- Boca Bay Croquet Club, Boca Grande.
- Boca Raton Resort & Club, Boca Raton.
- Card Sound Croquet Club, Key Largo.
- Cornell Croquet Club, Shalimar.
- Croquet Club at PGA National, Palm Beach Gardens.
- Deercreek Country Club, Jacksonville.
- Fleet Landing Croquet Club, Atlantic Beach.
- Gasparilla Mallet Club, Boca Grande.
- Hammock Dunes Club, Palm Coast.
- Hideaway Beach Club, Marco Island.
- Key Largo Anglers Club, Key Largo.
- Manasota Beach Croquet Club, Englewood.
- Mountain Lake Croquet Club, Lake Wales.
- Ocean Reef Club, Key Largo.
- Orlando Croquet Society, Orlando.
- Palm Beach Polo & Country Club, West Palm Beach.
- PGA National Resort & Spa, Palm Beach Gardens.
- Royal Palm Clubhouse, Homestead.
- Royal Palm Yacht & Country Club, Boca Raton.
- Seaside Swim & Tennis Club, Seaside.
- St. John's Croquet Club, Jacksonville.
- Stouffer Vinoy Resort Croquet Club, St. Petersburg.
- Tampa Yacht & Mallet Club, Tampa.
- The Breakers, Palm Beach.
- The Country Club of Florida, Village of Golf.
- The Hillsboro Club, Hillsboro Beach.
- The Windsor Club, Vero Beach.
- Useppa Island Croquet Club (Useppa Island), Bokeelia.
- Waterford Croquet Club, Venice.
- Winter Park Croquet Club, Winter Park.
- Yacht & Country Club, Inc. Stuart.

GEORGIA

- Atlanta Mallet Club (Atlanta), Lawrenceville.
- Brookstone Golf & Country Club (Acworth), Atlanta.
- Chattahoochee Croquet Society, Gainesville.
- Croquet Club of the South, Alpharetta.
- Early Hill 1812 Mallet Club, Greensboro.
- Frogmore Continental, Statesboro.
- Georgia Croquet Club, Williamson.
- Hampton Court Croquet Club, Hampton.
- Jekyll Island Croquet Club, Jekyll Island.
- Jekyll Island Resort, Jekyll Island.
- Okefenokee Mallet Club, Waycross.

HAWAII
- Kapalua Mallet Club, Kapalua.
- Lodge at Koele, Lanai City.

ILLINOIS
- Chicago Croquet Club (Chicago), Park Ridge.
- Wester Croquet Club, Rockford.

KENTUCKY
- Jordan Hill Farm, Richmond.
- Kentucky Rifle, Jug & Mallet Club (Louisville), Anchorage.
- Lakeview Mallet Club, Mayfield.
- The Ridgeway Croquet Club, Louisville.
- South Highland Country Club, Mayfield.
- Stamping Ground Croquet Club, Stamping Ground.
- The Summit Country Club, Owensboro.
- Trojan Farm "1875" Club, Versailles.
- West of England Croquet Club, Mayfield.

LOUISIANA
- Baton Rouge Croquet & Crawfish Club, Baton Rouge.
- Historic Spanish Town, Baton Rouge.

MAINE
- Belgrade Lakes Croquet Club (North Belgrade), Oakland.
- Kennebunkport Croquet Club, Kennebunkport.
- Ram Mallet Club, Cape Elizabeth.
- Toad Hall Croquet, Rockport.

MARYLAND
- Patuxent Croquet Club (Ellicott City), Woodbine.
- Potomac Croquet Club, Potomac.
- Underground Croquet Club, Kensington.

MASSACHUSETTS
- Blantyre Croquet Club, Lenox.
- Boston Croquet Club (Sherborne), Brookline.
- Carleton-Willard Croquet Club, Bedford.
- Chappaquiddick Croquet Club, Edgartown.
- Club Day Club, Edgartown.
- Coles River Run Club, Swansea.
- Edgartown Mallet Club, Edgartown.
- Fox Hill Village, Westwood.
- Lenox Croquet Club, Lenox.
- Marion Croquet Club, Marion.
- Menemsha Mallet & Racket Club, Menemsha.
- Myopia Hunt Club, South Hamilton.
- Nantucket Croquet Club, Nantucket.
- Naples Croquet Club (Naples), Acton.
- Sconset Croquet Club (Nantucket), Siasconset.
- The Country Club, Brookline Village.

MICHIGAN
- Harbor Balls & Mallet (Harbor Springs), Harbor Point.
- Heatherwood Hills Croquet Club, Grand Rapids.
- Lakeview Hills Croquet Club, Lewiston.
- Mackinac Island Croquet Club (Mackinac Island), Lathrup Village.

- River Place Athletic & Croquet Club, Detroit.
- Wequetonsing Association Croquet Club, Wequetonsing.

MINNESOTA
- Gull Lake Croquet Club, Brainerd.
- Madden's Croquet Club, Brainerd.
- Twin Cities Croquet Society, Minneapolis. .
- University Club of St. Paul, St.Paul.

MISSISSIPPI
- Natchez Croquet Club, Natchez.
- Poverty Point Mallet Club, Jackson.

MISSOURI
- Barrister's Lawn Society, Springfield.
- Creve Coeur Croquet Club, St. Louis.
- Spendthrift Circle Croquet Club, Kansas City.
- Wicket City Croquet Club, Kirkwood.

MONTANA
- The Backyard Club, Helena.

NEW HAMPSHIRE
- Hampstead Croquet Association, Hampstead.
- Sky Farm Croquet Club, Henniker.
- Stark Lane Croquet Association, Manchester.
- Strawbery Banke Croquet Club, Portsmouth.

NEW JERSEY
- Blossom Cove Mallet Club (Redbank at Harboridge), Sea Bright.
- Broadlawn Wicket Club (Sussex), Wantage.
- Hunterdon Hall Farm Croquet Club, Whitehouse.
- Mantoloking Yacht Club, Mantoloking.
- Pennington Croquet Club, Pennington.
- Rossmoor Croquet Club, Jamesburg.
- Roxbury Croquet Club, Kenvil.

NEW MEXICO
- New Mexico Croquet Club, Albuquerque.

NEW YORK
- Barneveld Croquet Club, Barneveld.
- Cedar Knoll Croquet Club, Sands Point.
- Champagne Croquet Club, Rochester.
- Charing Cross Croquet Club, Fairport.
- Clermont Croquet Club, Germantown.
- Eastman House Croquet Team (Fairport), Rochester.
- Gipsy Trail Croquet Club, Carmel.
- Glens Falls Country Club, Queensbury.
- Meadow Club of Southampton, Southampton.
- Millbrook Mallets, Millbrook.
- New Concord Croquet Club, New Concord.
- New York Athletic Club (Travers Island), New York.
- New York Croquet Club, New York.
- Pine Court, Tuxedo Park.

- Piping Rock Club, Locust Valley.
- Quantuck Bay Croquet Group (Quogue), New York.
- Quogue Croquet Club, Quogue.
- Royal Ghent Croquet & Yacht, Ghent.
- The Creek, Locust Valley.
- Triple Cities Croquet Club, Binghamton.
- Tuxedo Croquet Club, Tuxedo.
- Westhampton Mallet Club (Westhampton Beach), New York.
- West Hill Croquet Club, Camillus.

NORTH CAROLINA

- Bald Head Island Croquet Club (Bald Head Island), Raleigh.
- Black Mountain Croquet, Black Mountain.
- Carolina Meadows Croquet Club, Chapel Hill.
- Croquet Club of Etowah Valley, Etowah.
- Davidson Croquet Club, Davidson.
- Eseeola Croquet Club (Linville), Bokeelia.
- Fearrington Swim & Croquet Club, Pittsboro.
- Fishing Creek Croquet Club, Whitakers.
- Grandfather Golf & Country Club, Linville.
- Greensboro Croquet Club, Greensboro.
- Lake Winnekeag Croquet Club, Morrisville.
- Landfall Club, Inc, Wilmington.
- Linville Ridge Croquet Club, Linville.

- Pinehurst Croquet Club, Pinehurst.
- Richmond Hill Inn, Greensboro.
- Salisbury Croquet Club, Salisbury.
- Stoneridge Croquet Club, Chapel Hill.
- The Chattooga Club, Cashiers.

OHIO

- Firestone Country Club, Akron.
- Central Ohio Croquet Club, Powell.
- Cincinnati Croquet Club, Cincinnati.
- Little Miami Croquet Club (Cincinnati), Terrace Park.
- Maumee River Mallet Club, Rossford.
- New Albany Croquet Club, New Albany.
- Perrysburg Croquet Club, Perrysburg.
- River Rooste Croquet Club, Sidney.
- Western Reserve Croquet Club, Shaker Heights.

OKLAHOMA

- Tulsa Croquet Club, Tulsa.

OREGON

- Forest Lawn Mallet Club, Creswell.
- Nepenthe Croquet Club, Wilsonville.
- Portland Croquet Club (Portland), Beaverton.
- Willamette Croquet Club (Willamette), Independence.

PENNSYLVANIA

- Argyle Croquet Club, Glenside.
- Greensburg Croquet Club, Greensburg.
- Lehigh Valley Croquet Club, Northampton.

- Merion Cricket Club (Haverford), Villanova.
- Nittany Mallet Club, State College.
- Philadelphia Croquet Club, Philadelphia.
- The Waverly Country Club Croquet Association, Waverly.
- The Wickets (Bryn Mawr), Wynnewood.
- Walnut Green Mallet Club, West Grove.

RHODE ISLAND

- Block Island Croquet Club (Block Island), Barrington.
- Newport Casino Croquet Club, Newport.
- Newport Croquet Club (Newport), Washington, D.C.

SOUTH CAROLINA

- Arsenal Hill Croquet Club, Columbia.
- Croquet Club of Dataw Island, Dataw Island.
- Haig Point, Hilton Head Island.
- Pine Lakes Croquet Club, Myrtle Beach.
- Port Royal Croquet Club, Hilton Head Island.
- Richland Memorial Hospital, Columbia.
- Ryegate Croquet Club, Hopkins.
- Southern Rovers Croquet Club, Greenville.

TENNESSEE

- Cottonwood Bocce & Croquet Club, Franklin.
- Forest Hill Croquet Club, Germantown.

- Memphis Croquet Club, Memphis.
- Tennessee Valley Croquet Club (Knoxville), Harriman.

TEXAS

- Austin Mallet Club, Austin.
- Blessed Sacrament Academy, San Antonio.
- Dallas Croquet Association, Lancaster.
- Heritage Society of Austin, Austin.
- Houston Mallet Club, Houston.
- Lancaster Croquet Club, Lancaster.
- Northgate Country Club, Houston.
- 17 Acres Mallet Club, Arlington.
- The Croquet Club of Houston (Fulshear), Houston.
- Willow Brook Country Club, Tyler.

U.S. VIRGIN ISLANDS

- Bombay Mallet & Wicket Croquet Club (Cotton Valley, St. Croix), Gallows Bay.
- Tennis Club of St. Croix, Christiansted, St. Croix.

VERMONT

- Croquet Club of Vermont, Woodstock.
- Eagle Mountain Croquet Club (Milton), Westmount, Quebec, Canada.

VIRGINIA

- Burton Point Croquet Club, Charlotteville.
- Fieldcrest Croquet Club, Williamsburg.
- Fulks Run Croquet Club, Timberville.

- Great Falls Croquet Club, Reston.
- Green Oak Croquet Club, Providence Forge.
- Norfolk Yacht & Country Club, Norfolk.
- Richmond Croquet Club, Richmond.
- The Croquet Club of Norfolk, Norfolk.
- Wheatland Croquet Club, Purcellville.
- Virginia Gentlemen's Wicket Club, Chesterfield.

WASHINGTON
- Columbia Gorge Croquet Club, Skamania.
- Hollow Way Meadows, Grandview.
- Puget Sound Croquet Club (Puget Sound), Medina.
- Seattle Croquet Club, Seattle.
- Shilshole Bay Croquet Club, Seattle.
- Useless Bay Croquet Club (Freeland), Seattle.
- Whidbey Island Croquet Club, Freeland.

WEST VIRGINIA
- Buckingham Court Croquet Club, Lewisburg.
- Greenbrier Resort Croquet Club, White Sulphur Springs.

WISCONSIN
- Croquet Club of Milwaukee, Milwaukee.
- Oconomowoc Croquet Club, Milwaukee.

INTERNATIONAL CLUBS
- Caledon Croquet Club (Orangeville), Caledon, Ontario, Canada.
- Croquet & Cricket Club of Costa Rica (Guapiles, Limon), San Jose, Costa Rica.
- Croquet Club of Bermuda, Hamilton, Bermuda.
- Jumby Bay Club, Antigua.
- Langdon Hall Country House Hotel, Cambridge, Ontario, Canada.
- Lantana Colony Club, Ltd., Somerset Bridge, Bermuda.
- Lyford Cay Club, Nassau, Bahamas.
- Mulmur Hills Croquet & Bath, Ontario, Canada.
- New Banbury Croquet Club (Don Mills), Ontario, Canada.
- Northern Lights Croquet Club, Stoney Creek, Ontario, Canada.
- Royal St. Catharines Croquet Club, Ridley College, Ontario, Canada.
- San Miguel de Allende Croquet Club, Casa Loma, Mexico.
- Toronto Cricket, Skating & Curling Club, Toronto, Ontario, Canada.
- Vancouver Croquet Club, Vancouver, British Columbia, Canada.
- Westmount Croquet Club, Baie d'Urfe, Quebec, Canada.

TEN REASONS FOR A RESORT, COMMUNITY, OR CLUB TO ADD CROQUET
1. Croquet is one of the most popular backyard games in the United States. Forster Inc. sells about 300,000 croquet sets a year.
2. It can be a lifetime sport for both men and women since it is the only

outdoor sport in the world in which strategy is more important than skill.

3. Croquet courts are an impressive enhancement to any hotel, resort, residential development, or park.

4. Croquet can be played socially or in business settings, with varying degress of competitiveness.

5. Croquet tournaments and exhibition matches can be an excellent means of charity fundraising or other public service. The eighth annual Meadowood Croquet Classic at Meadowood Resort in St. Helena, California (called "White, Hot and Wicket"), raised money for the March of Dimes's "Campaign for Healthy Babies." The 1994 World Croquet Championship at Sonoma Coutrer Winery raised $150,000 for the Make-a-Wish Foundation, benefiting children with life-threatening illnesses.

6. Croquet, which can draw players with diverse interests, can increase community involvement. It attracts players who may not be interested in other sports because it is a game of thinking and strategy.

7. Courts can also be used for lawn bowling, increasing the options available to the public.

8. Croquet clinics and tournaments can spur publicity.

9. Croquet can pump money into the local economy through food and beverage purchases and room rentals for out-of-town tournament players.

10. Croquet can add five to ten years to the average country-club membership. Members who must give up golf will often stay in a club longer if it offers croquet. In some clubs, such increased membership has justified the cost of installing and maintaining courts.